The Renaissance

3 1472 70083 5766

Originally published as *La Renaissance* by Hachette Livre, 1996

Copyright © 1996 by McRae Books and Andrea Dué

English translation by Antony Shugaar

This edition published by Barnes & Noble, Inc.,
by arrangement with McRae Books and Andrea Dué

1999 Barnes & Noble Books

ISBN 0-7607-1264-6

Printed and bound in Italy

99 00 01 02 03 M 9 8 7 6 5 4 3 2 1

Michel Pierre

The Renaissance

with Denis Bocquet

BARNES
&NOBLE
BOOKS
NEW YORK

Contents

Andrea Palladio (1508–1580): Villa La Rotonda, near Vicenza.

Introduction

The word "Renaissance" means "rebirth." It would seem to refer to an extraordinary moment in history in which sunlight swept away the night, and lives based on spiritual values and the splendor of art triumphed over a dark, barbarous, and ugly past. This, at least, was the opinion of many people in the fifteenth century, who believed that they were living at the beginning of a new era. However, the term "Renaissance" does not seem to have been used at all until the turn of the eighteenth century, when it first appears in the French *Dictionnaire de l'Académie*. A century later, the French historian Jules Michelet gave the term its present resonance. The Italian poet Petrarch, as early as 1378, clearly felt that he was living in a new age which

The rather schematic view of nature typical of the Middle Ages gave way in the Renaissance to an attempt (beginning with Duccio, Cimabue, and Giotto) to depict realistic landscapes that reflected the order of the world. The generations of artists that followed, such as Gozzoli, accentuated this tendency even further, making the landscape an essential element of a painting's significance.

upheld the values of the ancient world of Greece and Rome, the only values that he deemed worthy of man. The same scorn that he felt for the centuries we now call the Middle Ages appears repeatedly in authors of the fifteenth and sixteenth centuries. Giorgio Vasari, in his dedication of the 1550 edition of his book, *The Lives of the Most Excellent Painters, Sculptors, and Architects*, to the Grand Duke of Tuscany, Cosimo I, wrote: "I have recounted the lives, the activities, the styles, and the conditions of those who revived the arts, which had declined into lethargy, and who then progressively elevated them, enriching them and raising them to the degree of solemn beauty that they occupy today."

Benozzo Gozzoli (1420–1497):
The Procession of the Magi, *with Lorenzo de' Medici, detail; fresco. Florence, Palazzo Medici Riccardi.*

Revival, rebirth, renascence—these words clearly refer to a new way of life. But we still need to establish the boundaries, the dates, and the events that comprise the Renaissance. Should we say that it began in the thirteenth century, with the sudden reclamation of new farmland and the construction of the great cathedrals of Europe, and end it in the eighteenth century, at the very dawn of modern times? Or should we limit the Renaissance to Italy between the fourteenth and sixteenth centuries, with its remarkable array of great artists and the masterpieces they created? Indeed, can we speak of more than one Renaissance? Perhaps we should stick to the common usage of the term, restricting it to the fifteenth and sixteenth centuries, while recognizing that its origins can be extended back to Italy as early as the 1360s, and that it persisted in northern and eastern Europe until as late as the 1650s.

During the fifteenth and sixteenth centuries, in the course of just eight generations, Western Europe transformed itself and then set out to conquer the world. In one brief century, Europe made up for all the losses of the

1

2

Sandro Botticelli, a protégé of the Medici, painted in 1478—for a young nephew of Cosimo—one of his most famous works, *Primavera* ("Spring"), the first in a mythological series that the artist was to continue after his stay in Rome; in it, the artist would develop the Neo-Platonic themes that were so dear to him. In this revery of a garden, the protective goddess appears in an atmosphere of wonder and grace, against a background of Tuscan flowers and a profusion of plants.

4

1. Pier Jacopo Alari Bonaccolsi, known as the Elder (1460–1528): Hercules and the Hydra; *medal in bronze with gilding. Florence, Museo del Bargello.*

2. Sandro Botticelli (1445–1510): Primavera; *painting on wooden panel. Florence, Uffizi.*

3. Melozzo da Forlì (1438–1494): Pope Sixtus IV Names the Humanist Platina Head Librarian; *detached fresco. Vatican, Art Gallery.*

4. Page from the Psalterium graecorum *by Aldus Manutius; incunabulum. Venice, Biblioteca Marciana.*

3

Black Death of 1348. The ensuing outburst of enterprise on the part of the surviving population seemed to bring an added keenness to the general desire for happiness, achievement, and fulfillment. The increase in population was almost a challenge to the *danses macabres* ("dances of death") of the earlier period. God had demonstrated His power to the terror of all, and while it was necessary to accept His will, it was also legitimate to pursue new horizons and new challenges. In Spain, this spirit led to the *Reconquista*, the reconquest of the lands lost to the Muslim Moors and revenge for defeat in the Crusades. In Portugal, two successive monarchs launched their caravelles on untried maritime routes in search of pepper and spices worth more than their weight in gold. France and England finally ended the Hundred Years' War and set to work building national identities. And Italy pursued its love of antiquity, its passion for the ancient Greeks and Romans, who seemed to embody eternal values and hold the keys to a renewal of the universe.

1

But nothing escapes the weight of the immediate past. In 1492, the year that Christopher Columbus discovered a "New World" to subdue with ruthless determination, and Granada defeated the last of the Muslims, marking an end to Moorish rule in the Iberian peninsula, Spain grimly lopped off a limb of its national heritage by expelling 200,000 Jews from its reunited territories. In the wake of the massive exodus, Isaac Abravanel, a dismissed minister of the crown, spoke out, addressing his people, relying on dignity to withstand injustice: "Let me be strong, and let us be strong, in the name of our faith and in the name of the life of our God, in the presence of the voices of the insulter and the detractor, in the sight of our enemy thirsting for vengeance. If he lets us live, we

2

For Piero della Francesca, the depiction of reality inspired by mathematical studies of perspective still tended to demonstrate the divine origin of the universe. The painter from Borgo San Sepolcro, who studied in Florence and worked chiefly in central Italy, executed one of his masterpieces in Arezzo: *The Legend of the True Cross*, in which we see a wonderfully clear example of Piero's determination to exalt the glory of his subjects while confining them to a sharply defined space, forcing them to stand out from the fresco in a luminous impression of precision and sharpness. The artist's other works confirm this tendency, and reveal his conception of the perspectival depiction of architecture and landscapes, as in the *Flagellation* or the renowned portrait of the Duke of Urbino, Federico di Montefeltro.

will live, and if he kills us, we shall die. We will not profane our covenant, our hearts will not quail, and we will march on in the name of our Everlasting God." At the same time, beneath the banners of another God, the Ottoman Turks were stamping out the last vestiges of the thousand-year-old Byzantine Empire. The great eastern city of Constantinople fell in 1453 and was reborn as Istanbul. The Islamic Crescent Moon rudely shoved the Christian Cross back to the very gates of Vienna, consolidating Islamic civilization from the Black Sea to Morocco, and from the Indian Ocean to the Balkans.

1. Piero della Francesca (1410–1492): Battle between Heraclius and Chosroes, *detail; fresco from the cycle of the Legend of the True Cross. Arezzo, San Francesco.*

2. Albrecht Dürer (1471–1528): The Four Horsemen of the Apocalypse; *engraving. Florence, Gabinetto dei Disegni e delle Stampe.*

3. The Siege of Constantinople by the Turks in 1453, *in a French miniature. Paris, Bibliothèque Nationale.*

The West withstood this challenge, and not with steel and gunpowder alone. The desire for knowledge led Western explorers to conquer the seas. One of Magellan's lieutenants was the first man to sail around the world. The printing revolution spread knowledge to a larger slice of society. The growth of banking and trade made many cities and ports the emblems of a new prosperity. The determination to equal the ancient Greeks and Romans led Europeans to surpass them. Brunelleschi completed the construction of the Duomo in Florence in 1436. Donatello cast his bronze *David*, finer than any statue of antiquity. In the churches and sanctuaries of Italy there was a profusion of works portraying a humanity that seemed more proud than submissive. Indeed, all good things seemed to come from Italy, to the point that it was soon a battlefield among those hungry for such a prize. The kings of France and the Germanic emperors faced off in a murderous and inconclusive struggle that lasted until the middle of the sixteenth century.

In three different fields, the early Renaissance found its highest forms of expression in Florence. In the field of architecture, Brunelleschi gave the new and unfinished cathedral of Florence, the Duomo, a cupola such as the West had not seen since the time of the Roman Empire. Brunelleschi had thoroughly studied the ancient Roman Pantheon before submitting his project to the town authorities, who were at first somewhat mistrustful, but in the end every bit as daring as he. In the field of sculpture, Donatello renewed the very conception of art, while the frescoes by Masaccio exemplify the new artistic ambitions of a generation that was perfecting the application of perspective, exploring new forms, and learning new and complex uses of shades and colors. The frescoes of the Brancacci Chapel, in the church of the Carmine in Florence, painted by Masaccio with Masolino, constitute one of his masterpieces.

1. Filippo Brunelleschi (1377–1446): The cupola of the Duomo, Florence.

2. Masaccio (1401–1428): The Payment of the Tribute, *detail (supposedly the portrait of the client for the series of frescoes, Brancacci); fresco. Florence, Santa Maria del Carmine.*

3. Donatello (1386–1466): David; *bronze. Florence, Museo del Bargello.*

4. Vittore Carpaccio (1460–1526): The Arrival of the Ambassadors, *detail; canvas, from the cycle of the Story of Saint Ursula. Venice, Accademia.*

4

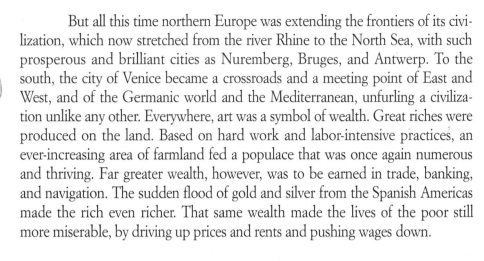

But all this time northern Europe was extending the frontiers of its civilization, which now stretched from the river Rhine to the North Sea, with such prosperous and brilliant cities as Nuremberg, Bruges, and Antwerp. To the south, the city of Venice became a crossroads and a meeting point of East and West, and of the Germanic world and the Mediterranean, unfurling a civilization unlike any other. Everywhere, art was a symbol of wealth. Great riches were produced on the land. Based on hard work and labor-intensive practices, an ever-increasing area of farmland fed a populace that was once again numerous and thriving. Far greater wealth, however, was to be earned in trade, banking, and navigation. The sudden flood of gold and silver from the Spanish Americas made the rich even richer. That same wealth made the lives of the poor still more miserable, by driving up prices and rents and pushing wages down.

Prior to the sudden flood of metals from the Americas that upset all economic equilibrium during the sixteenth century, there was considerable development in mining activity in Europe in response to the continent's shortage of metals. In central Europe, the production of silver increased five-fold between 1460 and 1530. The production of copper grew considerably as well, to the great profit of monarchs and merchants, among them the Habsburgs and the Fuggers.

Everything seemed to be going too fast. The discovery of new worlds, improvements in technology, and dreams quickly becoming realities—all provoked contradictions and a sense of anguish. The same people who were changing the world clung to outmoded beliefs. Ambroise Paré, the greatest surgeon of his time, made drawings of monstrous and mythical creatures, assuring his readers of their actual existence. Before him, Christopher Columbus, a learned and experienced navigator, believed, during one of his voyages, that he was coasting along a river of the terrestrial paradise. Jean Bodine, the first modern economist, wrote a treatise on demonology in 1580. These were not centuries of reason. Phantoms from the past reappeared and became even more powerful and there was a renewed interest in the fantastic. Thousands of people were accused of being sorcerers and witches and were burnt at the stake. Alchemists claimed to be able to produce more precious metals than the miners in the Tyrol or in the Americas. No prince could do without the valued advice of his personal astrologer. On the other hand, a few monarchs focused on the real world, laying the foundations of modern nations. They improved the administration of justice, and created stable systems of taxation and state revenue. Surrounding themselves with advisers and bureaucrats, they imposed the use of single "national" languages. The countries of France, England, and Spain came into being at this time.

3

1. *German goblet; Nautilus shell, setting in gilt silver; turn of the sixteenth century. Florence, Museo degli Argenti.*

2. *Hendrik met de Bles (1480–1550): Copper mine; painting on wooden panel. Florence, Uffizi.*

3. *Ignazio Danti (1536–1586): Plan of Venice; fresco. Vatican, Galleria delle Carte Geografiche.*

1

Lucas Cranach the Elder divided his career between Vienna and the court of the princely electors of Saxony, in Wittemberg, where he knew and frequented Dürer and Luther. His early period was a time of powerful, even violent works, such as the *Crucifixion*, while his later period was gentler and sensual, with subjects taken from mythology or the Old Testament. He repeatedly returned to the theme of Venus, an opportunity to express the beauty of the female body. Cranach's son, Lucas the Younger, later took over his father's atelier.

There were many different responses to the anguish and unreason stimulated by the world of the imagination. First and foremost, there was the pursuit of pleasure. Few eras were as permissive as the decades from 1450 to 1550. Eroticism appears in the literature of the time. Prostitutes, in Venice, for example, advertised special services and prices on printed lists. A few women claimed a right to pleasure, and many men demanded the satiation of their senses. The nude bodies painted or sculpted by Renaissance artists were more than just a reflection on the sufferings of the Christian martyrs, or the loves of the gods of Mount Olympus. The hint of a shiver that we can still sense in the flesh of a Titian Venus is the shiver of a real woman.

Another, quite different, response consisted in the new image that developed of family life and children. Erasmus of Rotterdam wrote ably of these new ideas. Marriage and faithfulness, and the happiness of growing old together; these were the powerful images that dominated the everyday existence of a growing middle class that sought its own system of values. These new values included thrift, domestic comfort, hard work, and the rearing and education of children. Parents began to love their children for themselves rather than for the fact that they represented wealth or security in old age. Thus, a new social class emerged that based its economic power on a way of life that established the enduring wealth of the countries of northern Europe.

2

1. *Master of Frankfurt (fifteenth century):* Celebration of Archers; *painting on wooden panel. Antwerp, Royal Museum of Fine Arts.*

2. *Lucas Cranach the Elder (1472–1553):* Venus and Cupid; *painting on wooden panel. Rome, Galleria Borghese.*

3. *Decorated Inkwell, 1500 ca.; painted terracotta from Faenza. Milan, Museo del Castello Sforzesco.*

3

1. *Master of the Mezza Figura (fifteenth century):* Concert of Women Musicians. *Saint Petersburg, Museum of the Hermitage.*

2. *Albrecht Dürer (1471–1528):* Large Bunch of Grass; *watercolor. Vienna, Graphische Sammlung Albertina.*

3. *Antonello da Messina (1430–1479):* Portrait of a Man; *painting on wooden panel. Rome, Galleria Borghese.*

4. *Paolo Uccello (1397–1475):* Drawing of a goblet in perspective. *Florence, Gabinetto dei Disegni e delle Stampe.*

2

1

During the Renaissance, the continuing effort on the part of artists to understand and perfect the laws of perspective led to a revolution in the spatial aspects of art. Objects set in space entered into a new correspondence with their artistic depiction, no longer in accordance with various forms of rough-and-ready empiricism, but in compliance with strict and precise laws, derived from the progress of mathematics and artistic research. Leon Battista Alberti, in his treatise *De Pictura*, offered an early theorization of this progress, to which Brunelleschi greatly contributed. Thus, the largely intuitive methods of Giotto were succeeded by a rational method that was soon adopted by the leading artists of the Renaissance. Piero della Francesca pursued the theoretical groundwork by publishing, at the end of the fifteenth century, his work *De prospectiva pingendi.*

On another plane, and unconcerned with everyday happiness, there emerged a new quest for salvation which the Catholic Church was no longer able to satisfy. An increasingly well-educated Christian population demanded far-reaching reforms. The Protestant Reformation, led by Martin Luther, was followed by the Catholic Church's response in the Counter-Reformation. However late Catholicism may have been in responding, respond it did. Its quest to express the new spirituality led to the creation of the Baroque form of art, which would illustrate the new ideas in stone, marble, and canvas all across Europe.

The Renaissance was a time of revolution. The fundamental change that took place was the emergence of the individual. The upheavals, anguish, and conquests we have described so far are at once the cause and the consequence of this. The hundreds and thousands of men and women who look out at us today from frescoes, paintings, tombstones, busts, or even printed engravings, are no longer symbols but real people. They stand before us, ugly or sublime, as nature made them. They claim an identity, a reality, a dignity, and a destiny that was entirely new. And they even claim a personal freedom, a quest for happiness on earth and the Salvation of their eternal souls. These images show us just how deep and far-reaching the changes that took place in the Renaissance really were. They laid the basis of the modern world.

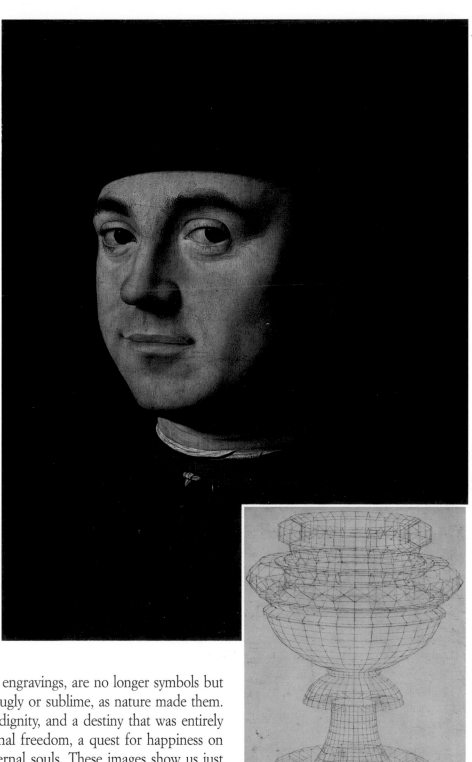

3

4

Gerolamo del Pacchia (1477–1535):
Ariadne Abandoned, *detail. Sienna,*
Chigi-Saracini Collection.

The Quest for Knowledge

The Passion for Antiquity

1

In the West, and especially in Italy, in the fifteenth and sixteenth centuries, the Greek language regained the standing it had enjoyed in the Roman Empire as the language of knowledge and thought. It was taught in the universities, where it became common to read Aristotle in the original, thus rescuing his work from the translations of the Scholastic tradition. Humanist scholars translated the works of the Greeks into Latin, making them accessible to a much larger reading public.

During the sixteenth century, inspired by the rebirth of arts and letters, by the masterpieces being produced by painters, and the splendid palaces and monuments built by architects, scholars wrote of the rediscovery of a mythical antiquity, an older civilization which seemed to embody all the virtues. Marsilio Ficino, Florentine poet and Hellenist, and translator of Plato, exclaimed: "This is unquestionably a Golden Age, in which we see new light shed on the liberal arts which had almost been forgotten: grammar, rhetoric, painting, architecture, sculpture, and music." This rebirth of the arts, so praised by his contemporaries, was based on a solid foundation of knowledge and developed into a lasting heritage. The legacy left by Roman emperors, Latin authors, and Greek philosophers had never been entirely forgotten, and neither had an intense interest in the arts of antiquity. At the end of the thirteenth century, when Giovanni Pisano sculpted pulpits in the cathedrals of Pisa and Siena, he imitated the bas-reliefs of Roman sarcophagi. When Andrea da Firenze, in 1350, painted frescoes in the chapter hall of the Dominican cloister of Santa Maria Novella, he depicted Cicero, Ptolemy, Euclid, and Pythagoras. And countless works from antiquity, some expurgated, others not, were found in convent libraries and thus contributed to the controversies within the universities.

2

However, it was not until the fifteenth century that this interest became an overriding obsession. Artists traveled to Rome to research and study, look at ruins, and seek out statues and monuments. Popes, prelates, princes, and wealthy merchants sought to outdo each other in the purchase of antiquities and manuscripts, proudly boasting of their possession. In 1447, the Vatican library owned only three works in Greek; just ten years later, the same library owned 350! In Florence, Cosimo the Elder laid the foundations for the Biblioteca Laurenziana, which became one of the richest libraries in Italy. In the same city, the Council of 1439 included the Emperor of Byzantium and the Patriarch of Constantinople, who attracted first-class Hellenists to their train. This was a decisive factor in favor of the study of Greek literature in the Tuscan capital, especially after the taking of Constantinople by the Turks in 1453, when some of those scholars, unwilling to live in a Muslim city, chose exile in the Western city that had welcomed them a few years earlier. About the same time, there was a revival of the study of Hebrew. Above all, however, it was Latin authors who were most popular with a reading public that, thanks to the invention of printing, could finally read the classics. Thus, works by Virgil were published in 546 separate editions between 1460 and 1600! Thus, more than 500,000 volumes were printed and sold, and it has been reliably estimated that each volume was read by four or five readers. So some two million Europeans suddenly had access to the works of the poet of the *Aeneid*.

4

5

NATIVITAS TVA DEI GENITRIX VIRGO GAVDIVM ANNVNTIAVIT VNIVERSO MVNDO

The revival of the study of philosophy, so much a part of the Renaissance, focused on the works of Aristotle and Plato, whose texts were once again widely read and discussed. Even so, we should not forget that, even in the Middle Ages, the philosophical tradition had been quite rich, and was anything but constantly limited to mining the "seam" of Scholasticism. All the same, the determination to gain direct access to the texts opened new horizons. The philosophical debate now grappled with issues that had previously been overlooked; questions such as that of individual ethics and the search for truth. Pico della Mirandola and Marsilio Ficino personify this new generation that had been nurtured on Plato, and which attempted to provide its time with new tools of thought adequate for the sudden widespread thirst for knowledge. Raphael, with his renowned fresco the *School of Athens*, joined the flow of artists who promoted antiquity as the basis for new aspirations. Here, we see Plato, carrying an edition of his dialogue *Timaeus*, and Aristotle, with his *Nicomachean Ethics*, embodying the ideal of Plato and Aristotle's reconciliation which so enlivened the period.

Raphael (1483–1520): The School of Athens; *fresco.*
Vatican, Stanze di Raffaello.

The Printing Revolution

During the fifteenth century, there was a burgeoning demand for the written word in Western Europe. Many factors contributed to this thirst for books. The demands of the current religious faith required a familiarity with the Old and New Testaments, various theological writings, and books of precepts for true Christian living. Merchants needed technical publications and travel itineraries. The warring aristocracy enjoyed epic poems of the deeds of knights and heroes and accounts of courtly love. Everyone—clergy, merchants, and nobility—was increasingly fascinated by Greek and Latin authors; knowledge of the classics placed one in a recognized elite. Reading, writing, owning a library: these were the hallmarks of knowledge, and of power over the helpless and illiterate masses. It is true that various new methods of copying allowed for an increasing production of books, which were now being printed onto sheets of paper, manufactured in greater quantity and at a lower cost than parchment. Invented in China as early as the second century A.D., paper was not produced on a large scale in the West until a thousand years later. Water mills, which powered the hammers that pounded the linen rags and hemp used in the manufacture of paper, multiplied in number. Paper, which had entered into everyday use, was used in all the various applications of "xylography," the art of printing texts and drawings by engraving them on a wooden board and then smearing it with a greasy ink. Wood wears down quickly, however, and new techniques were constantly being sought in the workshops of the wealthy cities of Italy, Germany, Flanders, and in the river valleys of the Rhone and the Rhine.

The crucial invention came out of Nuremberg, where, in 1434, a copyist named Peter Schoeffer, who worked with a certain Johannes Gensfleisch (also known as Gutenberg), developed movable type, which could be reused. Soon, cast metal replaced wood, a recipe was developed for a special ink, and a printing press was invented based on the wine presses of the Rhine valley. In 1457, in a workshop that had been set up in Mainz, their first book, the *Mainz Psalter*, was printed by this process. Ironically, by this time, Gutenberg had quarreled with his partners and lost control of his own invention. He subsequently won back his rights to the printing press, and from 1465 on, his print shop was producing growing numbers of books. The new technique spread with astonishing speed. By 1470 print shops began to operate in Paris, Florence, and Naples as well as in Spain, the Netherlands, and Cracow, in Poland. By 1480, there were already about a hundred print shops operating across Europe.

1

1. *Printer's mark of Simon Vostre, printer in Paris at the end of the fifteenth century.*

2. *A page, with an initial capital, from the "Catholicon," printed by Gutenberg in 1460.*

3. *Open cabinet with books, intarsia, turn of the sixteenth century. Loreto, Sanctuary of the Santa Casa.*

4. *Reconstruction of the print shop of Bernardo Cennini, printer in Florence in the second half of the fifteenth century. Florence. Museo della Storia della Scienza.*

Among the printers who began to produce and distribute this new object, the printed book, throughout Europe we should mention in particular the Venetian "dynasty" of the Manutius family. Aldus Manutius established a print shop in 1494, which was carried on by his descendants, and where many of the finest books of the Renaissance were published.

3

2

Lyon soon became one of the main centers of European printing. In 1530, more than 75,000 books came off the presses of the Tournes or Estienne print shops.

The printers who ran the presses worked twelve-hour days, but they already ranked as a sort of labor elite in this presitigious new field of endeavor.

4

The Quest for Knowledge

The Age of Engineers

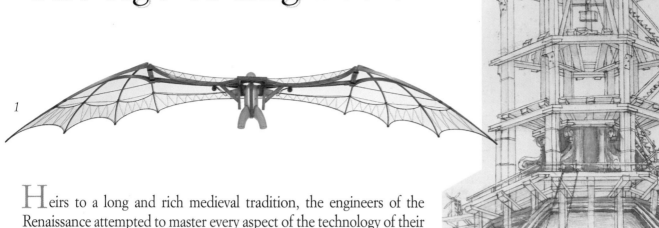

1

2

Heirs to a long and rich medieval tradition, the engineers of the Renaissance attempted to master every aspect of the technology of their times. They were inventive, skilled with their hands, and they had an understanding of each and every material. At once artisans and artists, they accepted challenges that seemed impossible, relying confidently upon their imaginations, blending intuition with solid common sense, designing—and actually building—siege engines, machinery and tackle for hoisting and lifting, complex gearings, ploughs, mills, looms, automata, bridges, locks and other hydraulic systems, mine shafts and galleries, furnaces, paints, and dyes.

Those who thus openly took on the challenges of the world of technology were equipped with a solid education in a number of fields and, in Italy especially, felt that they could carry out any order and solve any problem. Thus, the Florentine Brunelleschi, who served his apprenticeship with a clockmaker, built the cupola of the Duomo of Florence in 1436, proving himself a great architect and a talented sculptor. This kaleidoscopic array of skills, this mastery of multiple talents, was also found in Leonardo da Vinci who, in a letter dated 1482 and addressed to the Duke of Milan, Ludovico il Moro, boasted of his skills: "I have made designs for exceedingly light footbridges ... I know how to divert the water from the moats of a fortress to which one has laid siege ... I am familiar with methods to ensure the destruction of any fortress whatsoever ... I know how to construct explosive devices that can be easily transported ... covered wagons, impregnable and secure, armed with cannons ... I am ready to test wits with any architect, both in the construction of public and private buildings and in the diversion of waters from one place to another. And whether the challenge is to paint or to carve marble, or to work in metal or clay, I can produce works that will stand up to comparison with the work of anyone else, no matter who they may be."

What might have seemed like conceit in any other age, unbounded overweening pride, is simply a portrait of the man of the fifteenth century, ready to

The personality of Leonardo da Vinci was one of the great myths of the technology of the Renaissance. A swarm of inventions were attributed to Leonardo, only a few of which were actually original, when compared with such truly great engineers as Francesco di Giorgio.

1. The Flying Man; *wooden model built according to plans for flying machines by Leonardo da Vinci. Milan. Museo della Scienza e della Tecnica.*

2. *The lantern of the cathedral of Florence under construction; drawing by a contemporary of Brunelleschi, fifteenth century. Florence. Gabinetto dei Disegni e delle Stampe.*

3. *Jacopo De' Barbari (1440–1515): The mathematician Fra' Luca Pacioli with one of his pupils; painting on wooden panel. Naples, Museo San Martino.*

face any challenge and proud of the fact. Thus, the German painter Dürer was commissioned to supervise the construction of the fortifications of Nuremberg, and in 1527 he published a highly regarded work, *The Art of Fortifying Towns and Citadels*. By this time, however, specialization was beginning to become necessary, and no one could any longer claim to have mastered every field of knowledge and expertise. Michelangelo alone, an exceptional genius, could still claim to be at once a poet, an architect, a painter, and a sculptor. For the rest of humanity, the time had come to specialize in a field, as had the authors of the *Bergbüchlein* (published in 1505), the first book to treat the nature and methods of prospecting for metal ores.

The link between mathematics and engineering became increasingly close and fertile. Understanding of algebra developed rapidly, despite the persistence of some old errors, and the technical applications of these new fields progressed rapidly. Luca Pacioli, at the end of the fifteenth century, and Tartaglia, Cardano, and Ferrari in the next, contributed valuable mathematical instruments to Western science.

3

Scholars and Physicians

All the major towns of the Renaissance were also centers of scientific research. Research that was often marked by the medieval heritage, either with concepts that were too emphatically linked to antiquity or by approaches that were either magical or esoteric. Whether feeding on this tradition or breaking from it decisively, scientists certainly developed all their work in a decisive manner. Mathematics was renewed by the Tuscan Luca Pacioli, algebra by Cardano who published the *Practica Arithmetica Generalis* in 1559, and anatomy by Leonardo da Vinci and Vesalius (1514–1566). Vesalius, a native of Brussels, became a

2

1

In the countryside of the Renaissance, it was hardly possible to say that medicine had made much progress: charlatans of questionable skills continued to administer an old brand of science in much the same way as always. In the cities, on the other hand, the universities were educating new generations of increasingly well-prepared physicians. Medical education developed, slowly shedding the ancient prohibitions concerning the human body. The array of medicaments was enriched with new products, often arriving along the trade routes of the East, and the apothecary's profession became increasingly specialized.

professor of anatomy at the University of Louvain. He rejected the beliefs of antiquity, and relied upon experimental science, regularly conducting dissections. His treatise *De Humani Corporis Fabrica*, published in Basel in 1543, is illustrated with cutaway views that may have been drawn by pupils of Titian; these drawings contributed greatly to the popularity of the work, which was regularly republished right up to the end of the seventeenth century. Similarly, the Frenchman Ambroise Paré (1509–1590), who knew no Latin at all, but was a master barber-surgeon in his country as well as the chief surgeon to the armies and the court of France, was an exceptional practitioner. Although adept at practical applications and abstract theory, he was also convinced of the existence of demonic creatures. On the battlefield, he was unrivalled at extracting the shot of an arquebus from a wound; another of his innovations was to eliminate the use of fire-reddened iron for the cauterization of a wound, replacing it with careful ligature of the arteries.

Northern Europe, where Vesalius came from, seems to have rivalled Italy in terms of domination of the sciences. Krakow, where Copernicus studied, was during the sixteenth century the only Western university, except for Bologna, to teach mathematics. Nuremberg was a capital of cartography, or mapmaking. In Denmark, in the castle of Uraniborg on the island of Hven, Tycho Brahe built the largest observatory of his time, before leaving to pursue research in Prague. In Basel, in 1526, the chemist Paracelsus conducted his experiments, many of them marked by remarkable scientific rigor. And in that same town, Gaspard Buahin (1550–1624) did some of the most important botanical work of his time. Also in Basel, Sebastian Münster published in 1544 *Universal Cosmography*, analyzing a variety of natural phenomena, such as erosion, earthquakes, and sea winds and currents. The physicist Simon Stevin (born in Bruges in 1548, died in the Hague in 1620) was a noted specialist in fortifications, a famed mathematician, and an innovative physicist who was to demonstrate—among other discoveries—the impossibility of perpetual motion. Perhaps because it was freer than Italy from the traditions of antiquity and less dominated by the religious dogmatism of Rome, Northern Europe invented, researched, and created an economic revolution that shifted the axis of Western history from the Mediterranean to the Rhine and the North Sea.

3

1. *Hieronymus Bosch (1450–1516):* The Cure of Folly; *painting on wooden panel. Madrid, Museo del Prado.*

2. The Pharmacy, *detail; fresco from the end of the fifteenth century. Château d'Issogne.*

3. *François Clouet (1515–1572):* Pierre Quthe, Apothecary. *Paris, Musée du Louvre.*

A New Geography

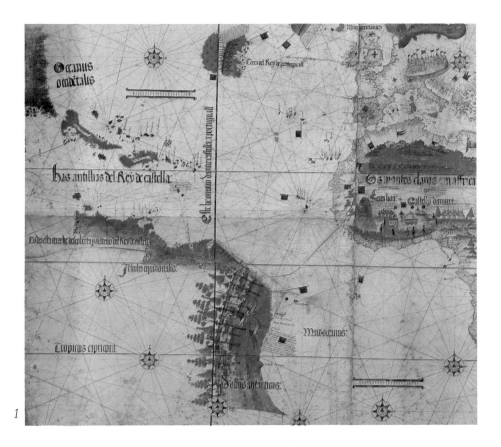

1

Beginning in the thirteenth century, the use of the magnetic compass and of *portolani* began to spread in the West. In the fifteenth century, maps were improved, and Christopher Columbus was able to make use of the creations of Toscanelli, for example. In the maps of the turn of the sixteenth century, as for instance in Catalonia in 1502 or in the map of the German mapmaker Martin Waldseemüller in 1507, there appeared a land, soon called *America*, to the west of Asia. In the sixteenth century, mathematicians developed new improvements in cartography, through the system of projections. The Flemish mapmaker Mercator developed in 1537 a map that featured meridians and parallels, and in 1570, another Flemish mapmaker, Ortelius, created a great cartographic compendium, the *Theatrum Orbis Terrarum.*

A period of a feverish desire to master various new techniques, the fifteenth century was also a time of striving to depict the world. The Middle Ages had produced guidebooks and itineraries for merchants and pilgrims, specifying distances by the number of days' march required, mentioning the legs of the journey and warning against dangers and difficulties. Some thinkers had also attempted to portray the earth, but more in keeping with theological teachings than the factual accounts of voyagers. During the twelfth and thirteenth centuries, cartography remained strictly symbolic and the few maps that were made were more concerned with placing Jerusalem in the most central location than with accurately showing coasts, rivers, and land formations.

With the development of navigational techniques, and the quest for new maritime routes, there was less and less room for symbols. Mapmaking became a simple, prosaic matter of showing real places. This led to the creation of the first *portolani*, charts of the coasts and ports that showed the location of

1. Catalonian map, known as the "Cantino," detail; circa 1502. Modana, Biblioteca Estense.

2. Paolo Toscanelli (1394–1482): Genoan planisphere; parchment, painted with tempera. Florence, Biblioteca Nazionale.

3. German measuring instrument; brass and ivory, fifteenth century. Florence, Museo del Bargello.

dangerous reefs and sheltering bays, steep cliffs, and islands. These charts also showed landmarks and seamarks, distinctive features that would aid in reliable navigation. The earliest *portolano* known is a Genoan map dating to 1290, showing the Mediterranean Sea; in the decades that follow come more accurate images of the Black Sea, the coasts of the Maghreb, and the shores of the Atlantic Ocean. In the fifteenth century, new techniques came to the fore; maritime charts were drawn against a background of lines at right angles: set on a precise grid, a sixteen-armed star, the *Marteloire*, indicated the winds and the points of the compass, useful to orient oneself in the entire navigable world. It also became customary to show, at the top of the map, the most evident direction, an arrow pointing north, as indicated by the pole star and the magnetic compass.

Most maps were made by Genoans, Venetians, Florentines, and Catalonians. Maps drawn in Barcelona, especially in the Jewish community there, were highly regarded, and were sold throughout the Mediterranean basin, and even in Bruges and London. In 1460, the Venetian mapmaker Fra Mauro, a monk from Murano, executed the first accurate map of the world in two hemispheres, based on information acquired from Italian and Portuguese mariners as well as from missionaries returning from the East and from Ethiopia. There was also a school of mapmaking at the court of the Portuguese prince Henry the Navigator, while the court of Castile encouraged cartography, this new activity, a key to the wealth of distant lands awaiting discovery. And a merchant/navigator of Genoan origin named Christopher Columbus became, bit by bit, during the 1480s, one of the most knowledgable connoisseurs of all the charts and maps and all the accounts of mariners, from southern Portugal to the Azores, from Madera to Iceland, and from Lisbon to Seville.

The Atlantic Horizon

While European mariners were quite familiar, from the thirteenth century on, with the Mediterranean Sea, the North Sea, and the Baltic, and the ports of these bodies of water were active trading centers, the Atlantic Ocean remained an immense and mysterious space, largely unknown and untraveled. All the same, to the north and to the south, it began to give up its secrets. The Scandinavians had for many years been sailing regularly to Iceland, Greenland, and the outlying areas of Newfoundland. To the south, the Portuguese seized control of the Azores and began to set out methodically to explore the coasts of Africa under the guidance of King Henry I, nicknamed "the Navigator."

In 1416 this young prince, just twenty-two years old, took up residence at Sagres, not far from

This map, drawn by the Florentine geographer Paolo del Pozzo Toscanelli, gave Columbus, who was unaware of the existence of the American continent, the illusion that he could reach the Orient by sailing west.

The Genoan navigator was the last representative of a fixed idea of medieval Europe: that of being able to reach the fabulous wealth of Asia described by Marco Polo, without crossing the lands of Islam, so as to form an alliance with Asia to encircle and, at last, defeat the Muslims.

CHINA
(where Columbus thought it lay)

North America
(which Columbus did not know existed)

JAPAN
(where Columbus thought it lay)

AZORES

EUROPE

THE CANARIES

MADEIRA

AFRICA

Cape Saint-Vincent, at the southernmost point of his kingdom. Overlooking the ocean, and tirelessly until his death in 1460, he organized a full-fledged research center devoted to the study of the stars, geography, navigation, and cartography. His ambition was to win for his country control over a new trade route to the Indies, which he believed could be reached by rounding the southernmost tip of the continent of Africa. He wanted to muscle in on the Italian and Arab monopoly on the trade in spices from the Far East and the riches that flowed across the Mediterranean Sea from the "silk roads" or the maritime routes. Under Henry, the coasts of Senegal and the Gulf of Guinea were explored, but the decisive voyages were undertaken later, at the behest of kings John II and Emanuel I, who continued Henry's work. The equator was crossed in 1475 and, in 1488, Bartolomeu Dias, commanding two caravels manned by sixty veteran seamen, was ordered to sail along the coast of Africa "all the way to the promontory where it ends." After a grueling voyage, he rounded the "Cape of Tempests"; upon his return the king renamed it the "Cape of Good Hope." That Good Hope was achieved by Vasco da Gama in 1497; after two years of sailing, he reached the coasts of India and returned home with spices, amber, and gold, worth sixty times the (enormous) initial cost of the expedition!

By that date (1497), however, Christopher Columbus, a navigator of Genoan origin sailing in the service of Spain, had already claimed (five years previous) to have discovered another route to the Indies, far quicker and more direct. After careful preparations, Columbus—under the title of admiral of the ocean sea and viceroy of the islands and lands that he might discover—sailed from Palos on August 3, 1492, in command of three caravels. After sailing due west for two months, and with his crew on the verge of mutiny, he landed on an island called Guanahani by its inhabitants, named San Salvador by the Spanish sailors (one of the islands of what is now called the archipelago of the Bahamas). Upon his return to Spain, Columbus displayed a few "Indians," some parrots, and a little gold. Too little gold, and the two expeditions that followed failed to bring back the expected riches from what was still thought to be Asia. Bit by bit, the idea dawned that the great navigator had actually discovered a continent hitherto unknown to the Europeans. A continent that appeared for the first time in 1507 under the name of "America" on a planisphere, or map, drawn in tribute to another navigator, the Florentine Amerigo Vespucci; no homage was made to the Genoan explorer, who had died a few months previous.

Christopher Columbus (1451–1506) learned his trade working for companies in Genoa, for whom he sailed the Mediterranean Sea and the coasts of Europe. In Genoa, he was also privy to a rich and venerable tradition of cartography. Moving to Portugal, he continued to ply the navigator's trade, sailing north and south along the African coastline. Bit by bit, the idea—which was in the air at the time—of searching for a western route to the Indies, became his central and overriding ambition. He was unable to secure the necessary support from the Portuguese monarch, John II, and so left for Castile under King Ferdinand and Queen Isabella.

1. *Pieter Bruegel the Elder (1528–1569):* Naval Battle in the Gulf of Naples; *painting on wooden panel. Rome, Galleria Doria Pamphilii.*

2. Portrait of Christopher Columbus; *painting on wooden panel, sixteenth century. Madrid, Museum of the Americas.*

The First Voyage Around the World

Following the great voyages of discovery of Vasco da Gama and Christopher Columbus, the greatest maritime adventure of the Renaissance—and perhaps, for that matter, of all time—was that of Fernão de Magalhães: Magellan. This Portuguese navigator who had entered the service of Charles V set sail in 1519 with the goal of finding a navigable passage linking the Atlantic Ocean and the Pacific Ocean, which Vasco Núñez de Balboa had discovered in 1513, after making an overland crossing of the Isthmus of Panama. To find this maritime passage would open, once and for all, the true route to the Indies, around the annoying obstacle of the lands that were recently named the "Americas." Setting out with five ships in October 1520, Magellan only commanded three ships by the time he laid eyes on the straits that still bear his name, on the 52nd parallel south, through which he sailed forth into the broad Pacific. In the spring of 1521, he reached the archipelago that we now know as the Philippines, and was killed in a skirmish with the inhabitants of the little island of Mactan. One of his lieutenants, Juan Sebastián Del Cano, continued and completed the round-the-world journey aboard the *Victoria*, which docked at Sanlúcar on September 6, 1522, ending the first circumnavigation of the globe by a human being. Of the 265 men in Magellan's original crew, there remained eighteen survivors aboard a single ship, little more than a sheer hulk, containing a cargo of several hundred kilograms of cloves. The incredible journey had lasted nearly three years, and the survivors had travelled 86,000 kilometers!

The two kingdoms of the Iberian peninsula by now controlled the oceans. The Portuguese jealously protected their spice routes, establishing trading posts on the coasts of the Indies, battling the Arab merchants in the

1

2

3

The Ottoman advance, which threatened to halt Christendom along the trade routes to the Far East, was certainly one of the factors that pushed the Christians to perfect new navigational techniques that might allow them to pass around the Islamic obstacle. A new type of ship made the Great Discoveries possible: the caravel. Relatively light and fast, with abundant sail surface, the caravel gave the Spaniards and the Portuguese a decisive advantage.

Seville, after Lisbon, became the world capital of the art of navigation, with its College of Pilots, and, more in general, the center of the flood of new wealth arriving from across the ocean.

1. Jacopo Zucchi (1541–1589): The Treasures of the Sea; *painting on wooden panel. Rome, Galerie Borghese.*

2. The port of Seville at the time of the Renaissance, with caravels on the river Guadalquivir; watercolor. Seville, Museo Naval de la Torre de Oro.

3. Map of America; fresco, sixteenth century. Caprarola, Palazzo Farnese.

4. Albrecht Dürer (1471–1528): Portrait of Catherine, mulatto slave of the Portuguese Bradão; *drawing. Florence, Gabinetto dei Disegni e delle Stampe.*

Indian Ocean, and making Lisbon a flourishing port where, according to a German traveller of the period, traders bought and sold "slaves, pepper, and ivory from Guinea, as well as musk, myrrh, parrots, monkeys, fabrics, cottons, and other products." Wood was sold there, as well, and of course sugar from the first plantations in Brazil, the only Portuguese territory in America and the only Portuguese territory to become a colony, since Portugal's scanty population prevented any such efforts in Asia. Spain, which had first established itself in the Antilles, took possession of Central America with the conquest of Mexico, and then conquered Peru as well. France, and then England, disturbed by the apparent Iberian supremacy, envious of these new discoveries and jealous of the startling wealth, set out in turn on explorations that appeared quite modest by comparison. Two Genoan seamen, John and Sebastian Cabot, in the service of the king of England, sailed to North America at the end of the fifteenth century. And in June 1534, Jacques Cartier sailed between Newfoundland and Labrador, on behalf of Francis I, laying the foundations of what would be French Canada, around the same time that the Tuscan navigator, Verrazzano, sailing from Dieppe in 1523, explored for the king of France the estuary of the Hudson.

4

Spanish America

1

The Spanish conquest of the West Indies led to the virtual extinction of the native population, who were decimated by diseases imported from Europe and by the abominable working conditions imposed by the conquerors. On Hispaniola, in just over twenty years, the native population plunged from one million to 30,000; labor in the mines on the mainland was equally devastating. The ensuing labor shortage was remedied by the Spanish, at the turn of the sixteenth century, by the wholesale importation of African slaves. A few voices were raised in protest against the frightful treatment of the Indians, in clear conflict with the Christian ideals that had supposedly prompted colonization in the first place. One such voice was that of the Dominican monk Antonio de Monesinos, which served as the inspiration for the work of Bartolomé de Las Casas.

Christopher Columbus's discoveries were disappointing. Not much precious metal, not much mineral wealth, not many spices—and so ambitions shifted from the islands toward the continent where, it was thought, lay fabulous cities paved with gold and silver. The *Conquistadors*, men of the petty aristocracy who had left Spain in search of glory and wealth, prepared expeditions, equipping themselves with funds borrowed from bankers and with moral support from the king of Spain who, through the *Casa de Contratación*, founded in 1493, laid claim on behalf of the government on all discoveries, as well as a fifth of the revenues that might derive from those discoveries.

In 1519, Hernando Cortés, leading a column of 600 soldiers, with ten bronze cannons and sixteen horses, landed on the coasts of Yucatan and, in the course of a few months, seized control of the Aztec empire and its capital Tenochtitlán (Mexico). Ten years later, Francisco Pizarro, with a third the number of men, succeeded in conquering the Inca empire of Peru by taking advan-

1. The Gold Mine of Potosí; *colored engraving from the end of the sixteenth century.*

2. *Funerary mask of the Chimú culture; painted gold. Lima, Museo del Oro.*

3.– 4. *Illustrations from the ship's log of Tonayuca, 1567. Seville, Archives Royales des Indes.*

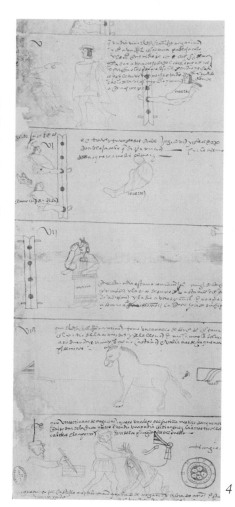

tage of a civil war that was rending the kingdom. The sack of these two empires provided the first cargoes of gold destined for Seville. In 1545, the beginning of full operation of the silver mines of Potosí, and three years later, those of Zacatecas, marked an enormous flow of revenue. The labor required was provided by Indians, pressed into slavery in their thousands and dying in almost equal numbers; this, plus the massacres of the conquest and the ravages of infectious diseases brought by the European invaders literally decimated the native population.

In a century and a half, then, more than 300 metric tons of gold and 25,000 metric tons of silver poured into Seville, as the "Manila Galleon" linked the Mexican port of Acapulco with the Philippines, delivering precious metals in exchange for silks and porcelains from China, luxurious cottons, precious stones, and pearls. The Spanish ships, which were basically solidly built, heavy-set galleons, slow but reliable (losses never exceeded 15 percent of a convoy), travelled the entire round trip from Veracruz to the Spanish coast and back in eighteen months. What they carried to the New World was usually a cargo of bales of heavy and fine cloth, wine, bacon, mercury (necessary for the processes of amalgamation used in the mines), copper, wheat, and weapons. This constant traffic, involving thousands of ships for decades at a time, this vast flow of money revolutionized the Western economy, prompting the development of certain regions and the impoverishment of others; above all, it led to a general rise in prices. There were also thousands of immigrants who set out for the Americas, perhaps 300,000 in a century; during the same period, the great convoys of African slaves began to sail, destined to replace the decimated Indian laborers in the great sugarcane plantations that sprang up in the Antilles and along the coasts of the Americas.

The Quest for Knowledge

The Crescent Moon versus the Cross

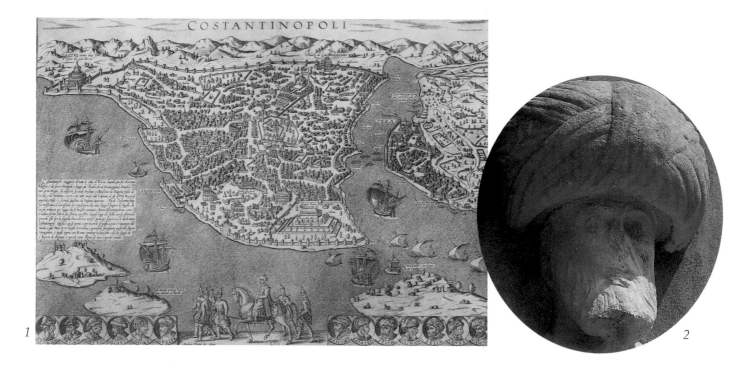

During the fourteenth century, the presence of the Ottoman Turks in the Mideast threatened the economic supremacy of both Venice and Genoa and compromised the very existence of the Byzantine Empire, which was being dismembered bit by bit. The Turks gradually occupied all of Asia Minor, then the two shores of the Dardanelles. By 1451 Sultan Mehmet II had gained the Bosporus, controlling the waters with his mighty artillery. Constantinople was now nothing more than the besieged capital of a vanished empire, finally tangled up in a long-encroaching economic decline. The acclimatization of the mulberry tree and the silk worm in Italy, and the enormously profitable spinning and weaving industry that resulted there, put an end to the ancient and fruitful silk privileges upon which Constantinople had long based its wealth.

The combination of the Turks' overwhelming military superiority and the Western Christians' inability to come to the rescue of the dying Eastern Empire allowed Mehmet II to conquer the city on May 29, 1453. The corpse of the last emperor, Constantine XI, recognizable by his purple boots embroidered with eagles, lay among the bodies of thousands of slaughtered defenders. The sultan entered the city, went straight to the basilica of Hagia Sophia and, after kneeling in reverence, scattered a fistful of dirt upon his head, in a sign of submission to

1. Plan of Constantinople; engraving, turn of the seventeenth century. Florence, Gabinetto dei Disegni e delle Stampe.

2. Head of a Turk; *marble. Venice.*

3. Ignazio Danti (1536–1586): The Battle of Lepanto; *fresco. Vatican, Galleria delle Carte Geografiche.*

4. Turkish miniature depicting the Christian ambassadors held prisoner at the court of Soliman during the campaign of Hungary in 1566. Istanbul, Topkapi Palace.

After the second half of the fourteenth century, the civilization of the Ottoman Turks underwent an exceptional expansion. With the creation of an efficient and centralized administration, and the succession of several ambitious sovereigns, from Murat I (1359–1389) to Mehmet II and then Soliman the Magnificent during the sixteenth century, the Ottomans managed to overturn the Byzantine empire, and to extend their rule over much of the Mediterranean Sea and eastern Europe. Their military might was largely matched by commercial success, thanks to their trade with the Venetians, the Genoans, and the French. Soliman remained the best known of the sultans whose power and wealth prompted both fascination and fear in the West; the mosque he built—the Süleymaniye—was one of the loveliest monuments of the period.

4

Allah. Then he ordered the transformation of the Christian sanctuary into a mosque, while at the same time authorizing the Christians to continue to practice their faith, setting aside places of worship for their use. The West was at once frightened of and fascinated by the power of the man who ruled over the city that was now called Istanbul. The Venetian ambassadors described him in their reports as "Great Lord, the most powerful on earth," and noted that he was wealthier than all the princes of Christendom put together. Venice and the other Western powers negotiated or fought, did business or waged war with the Ottomans, depending on the circumstances. In April 1454, the Venetian ambassador to Istanbul informed the sultan's court that the Serenissima intended to "have peaceful relations and friendship with his Highness the Emperor of the Turks." Likewise, Florence gave a lavish reception in 1587 to the envoy of the sultan. In the following century, the king of France Francis I enjoyed cordial relations with Soliman the Magnificent, whose many military campaigns from 1520 to 1566, against the eastern frontiers of the empire of Charles V, indirectly abetted French interests. These military operations brought Hungary and Serbia under Turkish control, but the sultan finally ground to a halt outside the walls of Vienna. To the east, he took Baghdad and Iraq. At sea, the thrust of the Ottoman war machine seemed equally irresistible; from land-bound warriors the Turks became formidable naval fighters. During Soliman's reign (1520–1566), they took Rhodes and part of Northern Africa. But, in 1571, an alliance of Christian fighting fleets (notable for its absence was France) under the command of Don Juan of Austria, dealt a terrible check to the Turkish fleet off Lepanto, at the entrance to the Gulf of Corinth. From that time on, a fragile equilibrium, punctuated by episodes of privateering, held sway in the Mediterranean, heavy with menace but equally rich in fruitful exchanges, and commercial and cultural relations.

3

The Birth of Nations

In the fifteenth century, the name Christendom was still applied to the vast assemblage of states of western Europe. These lands shared a set of values bound up with their religion, a certain vision of the world and God, and their clergy all used the same language, Latin. Everywhere, places were named similarly, after Saint Martin, Saint Michael, or Saint James. Dietary customs, feast days, beliefs and superstitions were identical over vast geographic expanses.

But beginning in the thirteenth century an awareness and pride began to spring up in belonging to a smaller, more closely defined community, tied to a specific territory. This pride also entailed a rejection of one's neighbors, nearby or far-off, and people began to define themselves as English or Catalonian, German or French (after the Ile-de-France), Norman or Breton, Florentine or Siennese. People distinguished themselves from their neighbors by their language, their specific customs, and a shared history. These differences were accentuated as certain monarchs, consolidating their power, contributed to the creation of national identities.

This general movement was extremely complex, and affected various parts of Europe differently. If an ineluctable trend seemed to lead certain monarchies to centralize all power into the hands of solidly established dynasties, another trend—equally important and lasting—kept vast territories fragmented into a

Of all the great sovereigns of the Renaissance, Charles V (1500–1558) was one of the most fascinating. Favored by a truly uncommon dynastic conjunction, which brought him the crowns of Spain, Habsburg, and Burgundy and combined with his success over Francis I in the imperial election of 1519, which gave him the lands of the Holy Roman Empire in Germany and Italy, Charles V ruled over most of Europe, from Spain to the Low Countries and Naples (without mentioning the nascent empire in the Americas). After living through the changes in the Christian world of the early sixteenth century, Charles V abdicated in 1556, making way for another great sovereign, this time a more distinctly Spanish one, Philip II.

European dominions inherited by Charles V, son of Joan the Mad and Philip I the Fair, and grandson of Isabella of Castile and Ferdinand of Aragon on his mother's side, and of Mary of Burgundy and the Emperor Maximilian I on his father's side.

1. Taddeo Zuccari (1529–1566): Francis I Receives Charles V in Paris; *fresco. Caprarola, Palazzo Farnese.*

2. The Arrival of Henry VIII at the Tournament of the Camp d'Or, *sixteenth century. Château de Versailles.*

3. The Defeat of the Invincible Armada in 1588; *colored engraving, sixteenth century. Geneva, Bibliothèque Universitaire.*

3

mosaic of principalities, city-states, and small independent kingdoms. France, Spain, Portugal, and England belonged to the first group; Germany and Italy to the second.

In the fifteenth century, following the Hundred Years' War, France seemed to be the most powerful kingdom in the West. It was by far the most populous, with no fewer than 15 million inhabitants (out of roughly 100 million in all of Europe). It was the largest kingdom, due to the political skills of Louis XI who brought down the Duke of Burgundy Charles the Bold, and his successors, who extended their rule over Brittany and subdued Provence, Armagnac, and Béarn. Still, this kingdom, however powerful it might be, had to contend with the rivalry of England and, even more worrisome, the nascent Habsburg empire. For nearly thirty years, three great Western monarchs—Francis I, king of France from 1515 to 1547, Henry VIII, king of England from 1509 to 1547, and Charles V, Holy Roman emperor from 1519 to 1556—faced off, formed alliances, and fought numerous wars. Charles V ruled over the largest empire ever to have existed, an empire over which, it was said, "the sun never sets," for it extended from Austria to the Low Countries, from Spain to Peru. However great his military and diplomatic genius, however, Charles V could not cope with his countless adversaries: the princes of Germany in the heart of his empire, the Turks on his eastern borders, the French to the west, and the English over the sea.

The Prince and the State

1

The birth of the great nations of Europe during the Renaissance radically changed the role of the monarch who, during the Middle Ages, had been expected to work above all for the unity and defense of Christendom. The long standoff of the Hundred Years' War between France and England and the *Reconquista* in Spain both confirmed, in the fourteenth century, the importance of royalty in a single country. This is the historical lesson of Joan of Arc, who wrote the following words to the Duke of Bedford in 1429: "Render unto the Maid of Orléans, sent here by God the King of Heaven, the keys to all the fine towns that you have seized and plundered in France … I have come here in the name of God, the King of Heaven, to expel you from the territory of France … And do not think for an instant that you will ever control the kingdom of France, under God." This prophetic vision encouraged peoples and princes to define themselves, set themselves apart from others, and to form the nations we know today. The universal dream of Christendom or the Empire could hardly withstand these new conceptions of the modern state. And these conceptions

1. Andrea Mantegna (1431–1506): The Family and the Court of Ludovico III Gonzaga; fresco. Mantua, Palazzo Ducale.

2. Leonardo da Vinci (1452–1519): The Hanging of Bernardo Baroncelli; drawing. Bayonne, Musée Bonnat.

3. Page from the manuscript of the Discourses *by Machiavelli. Florence, Biblioteca Nazionale.*

4. Bust of Niccolò Machiavelli; polychrome plaster. Florence, Palazzo Vecchio.

2

were being implemented by Francis I in France and Henry VIII in England, with a view to reinforcing the authority of the monarch, to create the tools needed by a centralized state, and to sweep away all obstacles to the royal will.

In France, Francis I focused primarily on increasing the number of officers of justice and finance (who were responsible for collecting the tax of the "tallage," so crucial to the royal treasury) as well as their clerks and assistants. Indeed, the Venetian ambassador wrote in 1546: "There are countless officers, and there are more every day. Lawyers of the king in every small town, tax collectors, treasurers, counsellors, tax and law judges…." An idea of the importance of the sovereign, his royal council, and the bureaucracy of the monarchy is provided by the *Catalogue des Actes of Francis I*, which contains 32,000 royal decrees. Among them is the enactment signed at Villers-Cotterêts in August 1539, establishing for the first time a modern state. Its 192 articles set forth, among other things, the rules governing penal procedure, the professional obligations of notaries and officers of the law, recommendations concerning the establishment of an official registry, the rules governing the various trades, and finally the requirement that all deeds, documents, contracts and judgements be written "in the French mother tongue, and not otherwise." The national tongue had become a fundamental tool of power.

That which was established in France was soon seen in other surrounding kingdoms; around the same time, a certain Niccolò Machiavelli, south of the Alps, called for the unification of the Italian peninsula under the rule of a single prince. But, as Montaigne was to write a few years later: "Is the truth marked out by these mountains, a lie to the world that lies beyond them?"

3

4

Machiavelli (1469–1527), combining in the field of political philosophy both realism and pessimism, appears as one of the great theorists of the Renaissance; he gave this field its first full independence from the constraints of theology. Born in Florence, he put his skills at the service of his hometown, until the fall of the republic in 1512 and the return of the Medici, who sent him into exile. In his *Discourses*, and later in *The Prince,* he set forth a new theory of the state and of politics.

The Power and the Glory

The Italian Model

1

For two full centuries, Italy set the tone for the West. In every area of economic, spiritual, and artistic life, as well as in table manners, fashion, and the way parties, festivities, entertainment, and celebrations were held—in nearly everything, the Italian model made itself felt.

Rome once again became the capital of Christendom, and nearly 200,000 pilgrims gathered in the Holy City for the Jubilee of 1500. Florence remained the foremost city in the arts, in thought, and in wisdom, a latter-day Athens where proud and respectable merchants and bankers joined the pleasures of the spirit with a sound business sense. Venice continued to glitter with its incomparable luster, set midway between the West and the East, in the heart of the Mediterranean's trade routes; and despite the inauguration of the Atlantic routes and the strained relations with the Ottoman Turks, the Serenissima remained a great capital. Genoa, rich in unrivalled banking expertise, was always a past master in the mechanisms of exchange, the relations between gold and silver, the transfer of funds. It was the bankers of Genoa, during the sixteenth century, who controlled the flow of money from America, providing a link between Seville and Antwerp. And what can be said of the growing power of Milan, and Naples, certainly the most populous of all the cities in Europe? And of the luxurious and civilized avenues of Mantua, Ferrara, and Urbino?

Architects, painters, men of letters, engineers, soldiers, and merchants were for the most part Italians, and throughout Europe, "things were done in the Italian style." A proverb of the fifteenth century put it this way: "Everywhere

Naples, which had a population of more than 150,000 at the turn of the sixteenth century and 230,000 one century later, was, during the Renaissance, one of the leading cities of the West.

1. View of the port of Naples during the fifteenth century; *painting on wooden panel. Naples, Museo San Martino.*

2. Raphael (1483–1520): Portrait of Baldassarre Castiglione; *canvas. Paris, Musée du Louvre.*

3. View of Genoa in 1481; *painting on wooden panel. Genoa, Museo Navale di Pegli.*

4. *Baldassarre Lanci (1510–1571):* View of Florence in perspective; *drawing. Florence, Gabinetto dei Disegni e delle Stampe.*

2

Baldassarre Castiglione (1478–1529) was the author of one of the most successful treatises on court life in all of Renaissance Europe and the following centuries: *The Courtier*. After spending much time in the lavish courts of Milan, Mantua, and Urbino, Castiglione entered the service of Pope Clement VII. *The Courtier* was printed in Venice in 1528.

3

in the world, there are sparrows and Florentines." In harbors and in construction yards, in the courts of kings and in public squares, Italians were present from Portugal to Poland, from England even to Egypt, where Venetian merchants received permission in 1552 to set up a trading post in Cairo… Some returned from this exodus, others remained in what had become their new homes, or stayed for many years, and not without prompting jealousies, rivalries, and cutting comments. But the style was set; even monarchs learned the language of Dante; Francis I loved to chat in Italian with the Venetian ambassadors; audiences clamored to attend performances of the *Commedia dell'Arte*. At the turn of the seventeenth century, Claudio Monteverdi wrote the first opera (*Orfeo*, 1607), adding a new and important page—in Italian—to the history of Western music. Thus, even though gunpowder, blast furnaces, printing, and ocean navigation were not Italian creations, the Italian peninsula succeeded in adapting, perfecting, and improving upon these and other inventions originating elsewhere. In the sixteenth century, the best printers were Venetian, the most skillful fireworks manufacturers were Italian, and the shipyards of Genoa and Venice were among the most respected.

4

The Power and the Glory

Rome and the Church

In the Middle Ages, Rome, capital of the Church, was no longer equal to the magnificence of its role. Shrunken within the oversized walls that had girded the ancient metropolis of the Caesars, the city was torn by rival families of the local nobility, each bent on securing hereditary succession to the supreme office of successor to Saint Peter on the papal throne. A versatile and brutal populace lived in the ancient capital, dismantling its magnificent ruins bit by bit to build hovels of brick and wood for the poor, and houses of stone and marble for the more powerful. During the fourteenth century, Rome received the ultimate affront: the papacy moved to Avignon from 1309 to 1377. During this great schism, scandal reached unheard-of proportions, with first two popes (one in Rome, the other in Avignon), and later three popes (beginning in 1409), each claiming ecclesiastic supremacy. Rome was now a city devoid of grandeur and prestige, riven ever more deeply by rival factions. It was not until 1417 that the Church recovered a fragile unity around a single pontiff.

From that time on, the city took an active part in the civilization of the Renaissance, for nowhere on earth did the memory of the ancient world sink its roots as deeply. The popes developed a passion for archeology, and fabulous collections of ancient objects and sculptures were assembled. The popes worked tirelessly to embellish the city, to provide the Church with the means to rule supreme, and—equally—to favor their own families, enriching themselves in a scandalous fashion. Of all the papal reigns, that of Alexander VI Borgia (1492–1503) was stained by so many crimes that, upon his death, according to the testimony of an eyewitness, "all the people of Rome came running in an extraordinary state of elation to see his corpse at Saint Peter's, eager to slake their eyes with the sight of a serpent, now dead, that—with overweening ambition and venomous perfidy,

The Popes of the Renaissance were at once commanders of the Church, princes belonging to the leading families of the Roman aristocracy, great patrons of the arts, and—in some cases—mighty military generals. Nepotism was common, and their power was often directed toward specific territorial objectives in Italy; thus, the popes were often deeply involved in the political struggles that shook the peninsula.

Giuliano Della Rovere, pope from 1503 to 1513 under the name of Julius II, was one of the great pontiffs of the Renaissance. Made cardinal during the papacy of his uncle Sixtus IV, he devoted himself, once he was elected pope, to the consolidation of the temporal power of the Church. In Rome, he encouraged the blooming of a new generation of artists, by giving important commissions to Raphael, Michelangelo, and Bramante. Many humanists saw in this pope, obsessed with grandeur, a symbol of the corruption in Rome of Christian ideals.

1. Vittore Carpaccio (1460–1526): Saint Ursula meets the Pope in Rome, *detail, taken from the cycle devoted to the life of the saint. Venice, Accademia.*

2. Raphael (1483–1520): Heliodorus Chased from the Temple, *detail with Pope Julius II; fresco. Vatican, Stanze di Raffaello.*

3. Ignazio Danti (1536–1586): Plan of Rome; *fresco. Vatican, Galleria delle Carte Geografiche.*

with all the possible examples of terrible cruelty, monstrous sensuality, and unprecedented greed, selling without distinction both the sacred and the profane—had infected the entire world."

Less roundly execrated by posterity, his successor Julius II came to symbolize those popes who were worldly sovereigns, rather than men of the Church, more concerned with glory than with spiritual reform, and more in touch with great artists than with the faithful. According to Michelangelo—who began working on the frescoes of the Sistine Chapel for this pope, as well as working on his tomb—Julius II preferred "the odor of dust to that of incense."

No sooner had Rome regained its standing as the capital of Christendom than it underwent one of the most terrible moments in its history. In 1527 the Holy Roman Emperor Charles V ordered the unseemly rabble of his army to sack the Eternal City. An officer who took part in the Sack of Rome wrote: "On 6 May, we took Rome by storm, killed about 6,000 men, plundered the city, carried off everything we found in the churches and elsewhere, and burned much of the city. In September, on our way back through Rome, we pillaged even more thoroughly, and uncovered a great many hidden treasures." When the imperial troops left the city, there were more than 15,000 dead—roughly a third of the population—either slaughtered in cold blood, or laid low by starvation and disease.

3

Venice and the East

Incredible city hovering on the surface of the water, wealthy entrepôt receiving the products of two continents and dozens of ports, splendid jewelbox jammed with art treasures, bordering the East, Germanic Europe, and the Italian peninsula—this was the appearance of Venice at the end of the Middle Ages. Of humble birth, situated upon an unhealthful lagoon, the tenacious and inventive city-state succeeded in mastering its limitations and turning its advantages to good use. Venice controlled the Adriatic Sea, its home sea, and possessed trading posts along the Dalmatian Coast and on the Black Sea; competing successfully against its great rival, Genoa, Venice traded with London and Bruges, boasted a population of more than 100,000, and enjoyed both maritime routes and land routes, leading into France and Germany.

The seizure of Constantinople by the Ottoman Turks in 1453 hampered Venice's freedom to maneuver and trade; variously, Venice signed treaties with the sultan, or fought him directly, maintaining a permanent fleet of war galleys while the Turks extended their power over the Mediterranean Sea. Venice was also undermined by the shift of major trade routes toward the Atlantic—where the Venetians were cut out—and the new Portuguese trade routes to the Indies, depriving them of profitable markets. Nevertheless, after a period of adaptation, Venice managed to re-establish its traditional links with the Indian peninsula and recover the flow of profits from the trade in pepper and other spices.

Alongside these rich profits from maritime trade, the city enjoyed earnings from the terra firma, or hinterland, where its landholdings grew from the end of the fifteenth century on. Venice had revenue from agriculture to go with the earnings from business and trade in its own products: woolen cloth, lace, leather.

Venice also specialized in the cutting of precious and semi-precious stones, the manufacture of soap, and the manufacture of glass. Beginning in 1463, Venetian glassmakers succeeded in producing "clear glass," and were thus able to manufacture mirrors, spectacles, telescopes, and vases, dishes, and carafes. Venice was also renowned for the work of its printers, who were the most skillful in Europe; among them was Aldus Manutius, who invented the "octavo" format, allowing the printing of small books, convenient and inexpensive.

To the same degree as Florence, and later Rome, Venice became one of the capitals of the Renaissance, with its palazzi lining the Grand Canal, and with its humanists and painters who were so skilled at rendering light, such as Giovanni Bellini, Giorgione, Titian, and Carpaccio.

The arsenals of Venice, where master shipbuilders constructed the famous cargo galleys that gave the Serenissima her domination over the vital trade routes, were, in a sense, one of the first great "industrial" undertakings. These establishments, in terms of number of laborers, and in terms of the very organization of the labor, were forerunners of later developments of modern industrial manufacturing. The Venetian galley, which by the fourteenth century was a ship that could reach considerable size, was capable of transporting goods quickly and safely, thanks to its oars and its complement of sails. In the face of the growing Turkish threat, Venice organized convoys of cargo galleys, escorted by warships, and commanded by a "*capitanio.*" In the sixteenth century, however, Venetian galleys underwent a rapid decline.

1. Vittore Carpaccio (1460–1526): The Miraculous Healing of the Possessed One; *canvas. Venice, Galleria dell'Accademia.*

2. Raphael (1483–1520): Venetian galley; drawing. Venice, Galleria dell'Accademia.

2

The bond that linked Venice with the East was, ever since the foundation of the city, so strong that it took shape not only in the flow of trade which, for centuries, ran almost entirely in that direction, but just as clearly in the religion, with the great Venetian saints—and first and foremost Saint Mark—often powerfully bound up with the East, as well as in the architecture and in the art at large. The basilica of Saint Mark's was built in the ninth century to house the relics of Saint Mark, and later rebuilt, during the eleventh century, on the model of the church of the Holy Apostles in Constantinople. The bronze horses which stood high over the portal

beginning in the thirteenth century were brought to Venice from Constantinople, where they had been transported—from Rome—at the orders of the emperor Constantine. Venice, then, drew its religious and artistic symbolism from the East, and even after the fall of the Byzantine Empire, continued—in a more complex relationship, clearly conscious of the need to dominate the hinterland, or "terra ferma"—to turn in that direction.

Gentile Bellini (1429–1507): Saint Mark Preaching in Alexandria; *canvas. Milan, Brera.*

Florence and the Medici

1

In the middle of the fourteenth century, just prior to the terrible ravages of the Black Death, Florence was one of the wealthiest cities in Europe. Its prosperity was based on the processing and dyeing of rough woolen cloth, imported from France, England, and Flanders to be transformed into fine fabrics with magnificent colors. Zealously safeguarding their manufacturing secrets, the Florentine craftsmen triumphed in all the marketplaces and fairs of Europe. The city's wealth also derived from other forms of textile manufacturing, such as the weaving of silk; the rich Tuscan farmland kept the great metropolis well fed, and the money-changing and banking activities brought in sizable profits. Because of reckless extension of risky credit—to the king of England, among others—many of the leading Florentine banks collapsed in the fourteenth century. In the meantime, the dynamism and vigor of Florence was such that the city managed to overcome the crisis that followed upon the ravages of the Black Death. Moreover, during the fifteenth century, Florence established itself as the capital of the Renaissance and gathered, within the massive city walls, the most unbelievable concentration of talent and genius ever assembled in a single metropolis. In all the areas of creativity that stimulated the creation of wealth—and despite wars, civil conflict, and the recurring threat of the plague—there was an unprecedented flourishing. Brunelleschi created a new architecture, Donatello did the same in sculpture, and Masaccio in painting. The Italian language, in the wake of the

In Florence from the beginning of the thirteenth century, the Medici family distinguished itself in Florentine business and politics, and, as early as the fourteenth century, it loomed large in the chief alliances. Closely tied to the leading families of the city, the Medici engaged in banking and trade, and took part in city administration. After the revolt of the Ciompi in the late fourteenth century, the Medici moved to the forefront of the Florentine political scene in the 1430s, dominating its political arena right up to the beginning of the eighteenth century. Cosimo, followed by Pietro and Lorenzo, established the dynasty which, increasingly, found its name associated with the name of the city, finally emerging as a veritable myth. The family recovered its power in 1530, in the context of the rivalries between supporters of the Holy Roman Empire and the Papacy.

decisive inspiration offered by Dante during the previous century, continued to develop in Florence. And the Christian faith found its most astonishing painted form in the brushstrokes of Fra Angelico.

This remarkable moment in the history of civilization took the living form of several families that dominated the town of Florence. These families fought often; at times one would destroy another, and they modified the urban landscape with their palace-fortresses with façades adorned with their coats of arms. Among those dozens of families, the Medici emerged as the most skillful and powerful. Cosimo the Elder, who successfully placed devoted allies in all the niches of the complex administration of the town, showed great diplomatic skill in preserving and developing the power of Florence. He succeeded in leaving his son, and his grandson Lorenzo, the inheritance of a full and uncontested, if indirect, power. The grandson encouraged creativity and the arts with his patronage, staged numerous festivals and tournaments, wrote poems, extolled the example of antiquity, encouraged humanism, and went down in history as "Lorenzo the Magnificent." He was, however, less successful in business, brutal in war, and he became increasingly unpopular among the Florentines for his high-handed gestures. His death in 1492 marked the decline of the Medici family, which would not find its power again until the following century, when an ancillary branch of the family founded a dynasty that was destined to rule over the Grand Duchy of Tuscany for over two centuries— a period that saw the rise of such new geniuses as Michelangelo, Benvenuto Cellini, and Pontormo.

2

1. View of Florence in 1480; *color copy of the "Carta della Catena"; watercolor. Florence, Museo di Firenze Com'Era.*

2. Benvenuto Cellini (1500–1571): Perseus; *bronze. Florence, Loggia dei Lanzi.*

3. Masolino (1383–1447): The healing of the cripple and the resurrection of Tabitha, *detail; fresco from the cycle of the Brancacci Chapel. Florence, Santa Maria del Carmine.*

3

War and Weapons

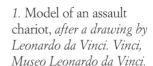

The two centuries of the Renaissance resounded with the endless clash of arms. The wars over the interests of great powers that focused upon Italy as the principal stake went on alongside the conflict between Muslims and Christians to the east and south of Europe, from the plains of the Danube to the coasts of Cyprus. Christendom itself was torn by wars of religion of a truly rare savagery. And that is not to mention the urban mutinies, the peasant uprisings, the sporadic revolts that were inevitably drowned in blood.

The fourteenth century witnessed the end of the Hundred Years' War; it also witnessed the outbreak of the new and interminable conflict set in Italy, from 1494 to 1559. Everything began in 1494, with the claims of Charles VIII, king of France, to the throne of Naples, as successor to Robert of Anjou, who had died sixty years previous. Charles made a military expedition to Naples, taking the town in 1495, after receiving enthusiastic welcomes in Milan and Florence. Later, however, tangled up in tricky reversals of alliance, he was forced to retreat to France and abandon his designs on the city. Three years later, his successor Louis XII erased the humiliation and retook Naples, but was himself soon forced to withdraw in 1504. Years later, Francis I was no more successful, despite the legendary victory of Marignano in 1515, followed ten years later by the equally legendary defeat of Pavia. After his capture, he returned to France in 1526 at the price of a humiliating treaty which he lost no time in repudiating, once he had been freed. His captor, Charles V, thus frustrated every French design on Italy, but was himself equally unable to outmaneuver French military might, while simultaneously forced to battle against the mutinous German princes, withstand the encroaching Turks, and contrast the ambitions of Henry VIII of England. For nearly thirty years, the three great princes of the West faced

1. Model of an assault chariot, after a drawing by Leonardo da Vinci. Vinci, Museo Leonardo da Vinci.

2. Bernardino Poccetti (1542–1612): A cannon factory; fresco. Florence, Museo degli Uffizi.

3. Engraving depicting a combination pistol-battleaxe, from the sixteenth century.

4. The Siege of Antwerp in 1585; fresco. Florence, Villa Arrivabene.

5. German harquebusier; engraving, sixteenth century.

6. Engravings depicting flint- and match-fired arquebuses.

7. Interior of a Tavern; fresco from the end of the fifteenth century. Verres, Château d'Issogne.

off, making alliances and betraying those same alliances; and none of the three was able to triumph over the others.

War, in fact—either despite or because of the wealth and resources of the combatants—had become both too complex and too costly for there to be a decisive victory, except for the case of naval battles, as was shown by the smashing Christian victory over Islam at Lepanto in 1571. Fighting could not be permanent, war could not be total, destruction and misery could not affect entire regions or subjugate the adversary, even if murderous folly was unleashed upon all of Europe. Thus, the Cambrésis region, just one example among many, was fought over by the Holy Roman emperor and the king of France, and ravaged during the 1550s. The town Cambrai was sacked in 1552, and then burned practically to the ground the following year by imperial troops angry at being unable to drive all the way to Paris. Two years later, on February 1, 1555, it was the turn of the village of Cagnoncles to be rubbed off the map, when French troops set fire to the church in which men, women, and children had taken sanctuary.

If the early Renaissance benefited from the end of the great struggles of the Middle Ages, the end of the fifteenth and sixteenth centuries was again marked by the constant presence of war in Europe, with profound technical transformations, such as the introduction of artillery and the development of huge arsenals and weapons factories. There was also a vast market for mercenaries, foremost among them the Germans.

The War Lords

If the idea of the nation-state truly came to the fore in the Renaissance, the belief that a prince needed to establish a standing "national" army was still not widely shared. And war, like trade and weaving, was the business of professionals, whatever their national origin. One highly emblematic battle was that of Marignano, pitching 23,000 German soliders and 8,000 Basques and Gascons in the service of Francis I, against an adversary the core of whose army was largely made up of 8,000 Swiss soldiers.

The lords of war, especially in Italy, the principal European battlefield of the Renaissance, were men under *Condotta* (hence the name of condottiere), a contract which established the amount of wages paid and the number of soliders to be recruited. These condottieri knew their trade, were generally loyal to their employer, but were caught in a welter of contradictions. Waging excessively murderous warfare meant cutting into their profits; eradicating an adversary meant eliminating a source of future combatants. The powers, cities, or states who paid these mercenaries knew all too well the dilemma of owing too much to their champion, of being under his power or fearing his betrayal, and thus falling under the power of the enemy. There was nothing disloyal in a condottiere, once a contract expired, serving the opposing camp. But it was generally thought poor form to actually switch sides during the course of a conflict, no matter the subtle interplay of loyalty and defiance, glory and betrayal.

If there was Gattamelata on the one hand (a statue still stands to his memory in Padua), unfailingly loyal to Venice, on the other there was the Count of Carmagnola, who betrayed the Serenissima to the Duke of Milan, and was arrested, found guilty, and beheaded in 1432. The best known condottiere, Bartolomeo Colleoni (he too has a statue in Venice, by Verrocchio) was commander-in-chief of the armies of Venice. A formidable leader, he managed his

NVS PHLIPPVS HISPANVS DESCOLARIS   RELATOR VICTORIE THE   RO3   1

2

professional career with great success and left, upon his death, a fortune estimated at 240,000 gold ducats, a sum roughly comparable to the estate of Cosimo de' Medici, one of the richest men of his time. Another fine career was that of Francesco Sforza, condottiere in the service of Milan, who married the daughter of Duke Filippo Mario Visconti, becoming duke in his turn. And Florence also still commemorates these lords of war with funerary depictions of them in the town cathedral, portraying the English mercenary captain John Hawkwood (Giovanni Acuto) and Niccolò da Tolentino, triumphant in the decisive battle of San Romano against Sienna.

4

The formation of national states put an end to the glorious era of the great mercenary commanders, but the most skilled soldiers, often from the poor mountainous regions of Europe, always found a welcome in the ranks of the armies of Europe. Despite the blanket condemnation set forth by Machiavelli: "Mercenaries and auxiliaries are worth nothing and are indeed quite dangerous; if a man wishes to base the safety of his state upon mercenaries, he will never be supported with firmness, for mercenaries are divided, ambitious, undisciplined, disloyal, brave with friends, cowardly in the face of the enemy; they neither fear God nor hold faith with men, and one does not defer defeat, save to the degree that he defers the attack; in times of peace, you will be plundered by them, in times of war, you will be plundered by the enemy."

War, in the Renaissance just as in any era, was expensive, and constituted a growing burden upon the finances of princes and developing states. The establishment on a perennial basis of a disguised tax that was to characterize the modern era, the spreading acceptance of bribery and corruption, was the result of the growing financial needs of monarchs, who had no other means of replenishing their dwindling coffers.

3

1. Andrea del Castagno (1410–1457): Pippo Spano; *detached fresco. Florence, Uffizi.*

2. Engraving depicting a processional helmet, sixteenth century.

3. Andrea Verrocchio (1435–1488): Bartolomeo Colleoni. *Venice, Campo San Zanipolo.*

4. Landsknecht troops being reviewed; German woodcut from the sixteenth century.

Scholars and Humanists

The fifteenth century was a special moment in European history; a vast new body of knowledge was acquired and horizons were opened that had never before been dreamt of. Everything seemed to favor that belief in a privileged moment for humanity, searching through Graeco-Roman Antiquity both for methods of thought and lessons of life. A set of beliefs were shared by a few hundred writers, scholars, poets, and men of the cloth, who wrote each other, debated, and in some cases even argued hotly. The great collective myths that characterized the Middle Ages slowly began to melt away—that of the Crusades, vanquished by the overwhelming might of the Ottoman empire, and the myth of legendary lands, replaced by the reality of new maritime routes—but there still stubbornly survived a dream of a golden age, taking form in the mythology of the ultimate refuge of Utopia. Utopia, literally "nowhere," was the title of a major work by the English writer Thomas More (1516), in which the optimism of the Renaissance encountered the harsh realities of the reign of Henry VIII. The book described the island of all virtues, where six hours of work each day was enough for the well-being of the collective, and where gold was used to manufacture chamber pots. François Rabelais offered a similar description in his novel *Gargantua* with its Abbey of Thélème, a utopian site more hedonistic than Utopia, and hostile to all restrictive moralism, where the ruling motto was *Fay ce que vouldras* — or "Do what you like." In each case, however, the dream was to control the life of the collective. An idea that was, in a sense, anachronistic, in that the revolutionary core of the Renaissance was linked specifically to the emergence of the idea of the individual, the recognition of what the Italians called *"virtù,"* i.e., energy, intelligence, the courage to challenge and to build one's own destiny, as the humanist Pontano put it with his declaration, "I have created myself." A form of optimistic self-determination that appears again in the work of Erasmus who felt that man could achieve "true good" through a path of personal development, "an inclination, a profoundly instinctive propensity toward Good."

After the first few generations of humanists, mainly Italian, writers and thinkers from northern Europe took their place in this flourishing school, including the English thinker Thomas More (1487–1535). In the midst of a profound crisis of Christianity, in a world riven by political quarrels, he offered a meditation upon Christian humanism that led him to construct a Platonic republic, Utopia, where man could discover the mechanisms that tied him to the world, and which he could use to obtain true freedom.

1

2

Erasmus of Rotterdam (1466–1536), of humble birth, studied at the chapter school of St. Lebuin's in Deventer. At first a monk, he was ordained as a priest in 1492. By the end of the fifteenth century he was considered a major thinker. He later traveled throughout Europe, meeting the leading humanists of his time, and writing essays that were increasingly popular, among them *In Praise of Folly*, the *Adages*, and the *Colloquia Familiaria*. The end of his life was marked by the dilemma of a humanist faithful to the church and confronted by the convulsions of the Reformation.

4

All the same, humanist culture, steeped as it was in Greek and Latin, based on knowledge of the works of Plato and Aristotle, open to the esoteric and to alchemy, and seeking the impossible mastery of all human knowledge, distanced itself from the realities of life, the feelings of ordinary people, and set itself on a collision course with public opinion. It provoked rejection, such as that of Savonarola, himself an eminent humanist, who exclaimed in 1492: "When you ask whether the sciences discovered by the pagans are necessary to the Christian religion, I think that one must reply that they are quite simply the least necessary thing that could exist, since it is possible to be a Christian and live as a Christian without them .... philosophy, which is nothing more than a handmaiden, has seduced like some prostitute a great number of men of the Church."

1. Jan Gossaert, known as Mabuse (1470–1533): Portrait of Thomas More; *painting on wooden panel. Aix-en-Provence, Musée Granet.*

2. Illustration depicting the city of Utopia.

3. Hieronymus Bosch (1450–1516): The Ship of Fools; *painting on wooden panel. Paris, Musée du Louvre.*

4. Holbein the Younger (1497–1543): Portrait of Erasmus of Rotterdam Writing; *painting on wooden panel. Paris, Musée du Louvre.*

The Power and the Glory

Humanist thought was often tied to the development of national languages. This movement was first announced in Italy with the great work of Dante, truly the founder of the Italian language; in the Italian peninsula, during the Renaissance, the vernacular took its place alongside Latin. Thus, as great an artist as Michelangelo wrote his poetry in Italian. In the rest of Europe, the movement was slower, but no less profound and decisive. In France, Rabelais expressed his vision of the society of his time in the French language, not Latin. The humanists worked also to make the Bible accessible to ordinary Christians by translating it into the vernacular tongue. Luther, in Germany, gave all the support of his authority to this movement, which meant to place the Sacred Scripture at the heart of Christian thought, in order to make religion closer to man and man's new sensibility, which could no longer be satisfied with the distance imposed by medieval religion. College education likewise confirmed this movement toward the spread of the various national languages, a movement that took place in every land; for instance, during the following century, in England, with Shakespeare.

Vittore Carpaccio (1460–1526): Saint Augustine in his Study; *canvas. Venice, Scuola di San Giorgio degli Schiavoni.*

Artists and Artisans

1

The Renaissance also owed its exceptional artistic vitality to the prosperity of the time and the spreading system of patronage. Artists crisscrossed all Italy in response to invitations to come and work in this or that city, for the glory of a family, a prince, or a religious institution. Later, during the sixteenth century, because of the growing wealth of clients, artists were increasingly well paid, and leading families, such as the Medici, tied their names to the production of the geniuses of the time.

In the fifteenth century, appreciation for a work of art and the reputation of an artist was based first and foremost upon manual skill. Placed very young as apprentices, in some cases at the age of seven, would-be artists would be trained to the profession in ateliers, working first of all as helpers assigned to do unrewarding tasks, then as students, and then as assitants to the master artist or craftsman, before they could hope to set up in business for themselves. These ateliers also produced pieces of inlaid work; signs for shopkeepers; emblems for guilds; hope chests to hold the trousseaux of young brides of the local nobility; earthenware tiling, soup tureens, salt cellars, and other objects to adorn the table; ornamentations and crests for helmets; emblems; and decorations for Carnival. These things were typical of Italy; elsewhere there were also craftsmen who specialized in small indoor clocks and the very earliest pocketwatches, made in Nuremberg. Invented by the clockmaker Peter Henlein, who replaced the older system of weights and counterweights with a series of small springs, they were ovoid in shape and were dubbed "eggs of Nuremberg"; they were worn around the neck on a gold chain.

In these ateliers, the talents of a young man (young women were exceedingly rare in these professions) would be carefully evaluated, and if he qualified, he would be set on the path to the noble profession of painter, the top of the totem pole in terms of prestige. It was thus, accord-

2

ing to Vasari, that Andrea del Sarto's talent was first noted: "At the age of seven, he was taken out of school, where he had been studying to read and write, and apprenticed with a goldsmith. There, his instincts led him to draw much more than to handle the tools for working silver and gold. The Florentine painter Gian Barile, however unmannerly and vulgar, recognized the young boy's talent for drawing and took him as an apprentice, and taught him to paint."

The sixteenth century, in fact, marked a break between the profession of artisan and that of artist. It was not possible to be an artist without the skills of an artisan, but being recognized as a painter or a sculptor opened the doors of the palace, allowing one to become wealthy and to gain access to the places that matter in society. No client who commissioned a fresco or painting on wood, especially in Italy, would ever object to seeing a self-portrait of the artist upon the finished product. And that is how art experts at Florence know, as if from photographs, the features of Botticelli (*Adoration of the Magi*, Uffizi), Filippino Lippi (fresco of the Brancacci Chapel), Benozzo Gozzoli (*Procession of the Magi*, Chapel of Palazzo Medici Riccardi), Domenico Ghirlandaio (Tornabuoni Chapel, Santa Maria Novella, and twice in the chapel of the Sassetti family in the church of Santa Trinita).

3

4

1. Lorenzo Ghiberti (1378–1455): self portrait, detail from a panel of the Porta del Paradiso, or Door of Paradise; gilt bronze. Florence, Baptistery.

2. Giovanni Girolamo Savoldo (1480–1548): self portrait in front of a mirror; canvas. Paris, Musée du Louvre.

3. Federico Zuccari (1540–1609): Monsignor Borghini giving instructions to the artist for the paintings in the cupola of the Duomo of Florence; *drawing. Florence, Gabinetto dei Disegni e delle Stampe.*

4. Giovan Maria Butteri (sixteenth century): The glass workshop, *detail; panel of a cabinet. Florence, Palazzo Vecchio, studiolo of Francesco I.*

5. Vase made of rock crystal, in the shape of a bird, late sixteenth century. Florence, Museo degli Argenti.

6. Small Parisian coffer; mother-of-pearl, gilt silver, precious and semi-precious stones, sixteenth century. Mantua. Museo Diocesano.

6

The Power and the Glory

The Age of Genius

Unquestionably, at no time in the history of the West has there been such a profusion of masterpieces. In painting, Masaccio, Leonardo da Vinci, Piero della Francesca, Michelangelo, Raphael, and Titian (Italy), Dürer, Holbein, and Cranach (Germany), Van Eyck and Memling (Flanders). And what of the hundreds of palaces that sprang up across Europe? The Palladian villas, whose style would influence architecture for centuries to come? The enormous constructions, such as Saint Peter's in Rome? The incredible conjunction of princely wealth, artisans' skill, and the genius of a few dozen artists—all lay at the origin of this flourishing of the arts.

Of all these Renaissance geniuses two figures emerged in Florence that towered over all the others—Leonardo da Vinci and Michelangelo. Both were endowed with multiple talents, and were extraordinary beings working in a remarkable state of solitude, almost of anguish. *La Gioconda*, or *The Mona Lisa,* (1506) for Leonardo and the frescoes of the Sistine Chapel (beginning in 1512) for Michelangleo, remain the absolute masterpieces, created during lives punctuated by moments of discouragement and depression. If Leonardo, according to a witness, "seemed to tremble each time he began to paint," then Michelangelo put it this way: "Painting and sculpture, hard work and great responsibility have ruined my health, which is going from bad to worse. It would have been better for me if, in my youth, I had dedicated myself to making matches."

Giorgione, and the long-lived Titian (1490–1576), succeeded in capturing the ineffable light of Venice, and were just as admired as the Florentine painters, to the point that it is said that Charles V knelt to pick up a paintbrush that Titian had dropped while painting the emperor's portrait. In Germany, Dürer was the painter of fine details and of the psychology of facial features. These qualities were shared by the Flemish painters, who added their mastery of oil painting and their remarkable sense of atmospheric perspective. The architects, from Brunelleschi to Alberti and Palladio, blended sheer mental genius with a mastery of manual skills and a thorough knowledge of stones, woods, styles, orders, cements, and mortars. This complex body of knowledge was set forth by Palladio in four great books of architecture published in Venice in 1570, where he expressed his aim to seek out beauty "as the product of form and the correspondence of all the parts, i.e., of the parts among themselves, and of all the parts to the whole, so that the edifice might appear as a complete and well-finished body, in which every member goes nicely with the others and where all of the members are necessary to what one had set out to accomplish."

1

Michelangelo was certainly one of the last great universal geniuses of the Renaissance. His career, divided between the Florence of Lorenzo the Magnificent and the Rome of Pope Pius IV, marked a high point in the conjunction of an exceptional talent and a set of enlightened clients. Piero della Francesca, his predecessor, had limited his genius to the art of painting, and the generations that followed Michelangelo lost his versatility and devoted their energies to a single field.

1. Michelangelo (1475–1564): Atlas; *marble. Florence, Accademia.*

2. Leonardo da Vinci (1452–1519): Sketch of the proportions of the human body; *drawing. Venice, Accademia.*

3. Piero della Francesca (1410–1492): The Flagellation; *painting on wooden panel. Urbino, Palazzo Ducale.*

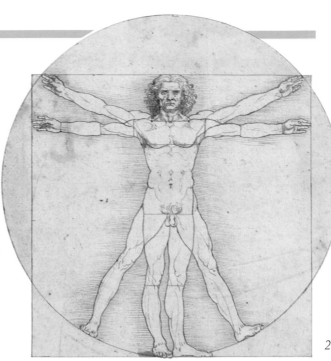

2

3

The Power and the Glory

The art of the Renaissance, aside from its fascination with the rediscovery and reinterpretation of the works of antiquity, was particularly keen on the themes of mythology, by this point treating them side by side with religious subjects. There was also a distinct passion for the portrayal of the female body, landscapes,

nature and man's relationship with nature. Often, one could see in the subjects treated depictions of the society of the period, and relatively discreet placement of the clients of the work or even of the artist himself at the easel. *Sacred Love and Profane Love* by Titian is one of the emblematic artworks of the

sixteenth century. The artist, who worked in Venice alongside Gentile Bellini and Giorgione beginning at the turn of the century, later moved—thanks to the favor shown him by Charles V—from Rome to Augsburg, and then back to Venice, leaving many of the most outstanding paintings of a turbulent century that he

experienced from start to finish.
We find in him much of the character of
his masters, but with perhaps a more
finely honed sense of balance and
composition. The painter, with his
remarkable colors, meant to give new life
to the myths of antiquity, and to exalt the
female nude.

Titian (1490–1576): Sacred Love
and Profane Love; *canvas. Rome,
Galleria Borghese.*

A Better Life

Merchants and Bankers

The Italian businessmen who invented capitalism during the fifteenth and sixteenth centuries demonstrated a remarkable understanding of economics and astonishing technical skills. They seized every opportunity to earn a profit, but on the whole they stuck each to his specialty. They could rely upon books called the *Pratiche di Mercatura*, which were manuals or guides providing useful information on the conduct of business, including the price of products, the distances separating towns and cities, rates of exchange, and correspondences in weights and measures. These businessmen founded their own schools, far from the madding—and to their ears, useless—debates of the universities. These early business schools offered practical learning, concrete and in touch with the realities of the world. In Florence, many thousands of young people studied in these schools, before beginning apprenticeships in distant branch offices of a bank or trading company. In Genoa, students in the business schools chiefly studied the banking techniques that gave the city, from the fourteenth century on, a virtually unrivalled dominance over the European marketplace, making the period 1550–1650 the "century of the Genoan bankers." Indeed, the names of all the great merchant families of Genoa appear in the *Arquivio de Protocolos*, the notary archives of Seville, the capital of commerce on the Atlantic Ocean. Communities of Venetian merchants sprang up everywhere along the shores of the Mediterranean and even in various trading posts along the Red Sea. While Italy remained a fundamental component of these new markets, Germany, England, Flanders, and soon enough, the Low Countries all boasted their own trading dynasties. Founded in the fourteenth century, the house of Fugger, from Augsburg, in Bavaria, began by trading in spicies, silks, and fine cloths, taking advantage of their city's strategic location. In 1473, Jakob Fugger, known as "Jakob the Rich," took over and established a working partnership with the Habsburgs, becoming their chief banker and gradually seizing control of the silver mines of Tyrol and Hungary; in time, he was accorded a monopoly over the sale of salt in all of Germany. His true hour of glory came with the election of Charles of Habsburg, who became Charles V in 1519. Out of the 850,000 florins required to swing this election, 540,000 were loaned by the

Money handling and banking progressed greatly during the Renaissance. The use of letters of exchange, the forerunners of modern checks, became common, and the chief currencies—the Florentine florin, the German thaler, and the Venetian ducat—were accepted in marketplaces all over the continent. The shortage of gold and silver was slaked, in the first few years of the sixteenth century, by the flow of metals from the Americas.

3

4

1. Venetian safe; wood and iron, sixteenth century. Florence, Palazzo Davanzati.

2. Jakob Fugger in his office; colored drawing, 1518. Braunschweig, Herzog Anton Ulrich Museum.

3. Fra' Angelico (1395–1455): A miracle of Saint Nicholas, detail; painting on wooden panel. Vatican, Art Gallery.

4. Quentin Metsys (1466–1530): The Money Changer and His Wife; painting on wooden panel. Paris, Musée du Louvre.

Fuggers. The new monarch demonstrated his grateful recognition by according new privileges to that banking family, new concessions, and new mines.

More than ever before, merchants were closely associated with the growth of cities and harbors. In Antwerp, during the sixteenth century—along the new and burgeoning axis of Western trade—hundreds of trading companies set up branch offices. And this Internationale of merchants and entrepreneurs was by now officially recognized by the Church, which had long viewed with a jaundiced eye earnings based upon the passage of time (e.g. interest-bearing loans), since the passage of time was the province of the Lord God alone. This ecclesiastical time, punctuated by the tolling of church bells, respectful of the changing seasons, was accompanied, and sometimes replaced, by the time kept by mechanical clocks, now a nearly universal presence. These clocks neatly sectioned time into hours of uniform length, the perfect medium for industry and trade. With this mastery of a new sort of time, the merchants and entrepreneurs of the Renaissance began to write a new page in the history of human endeavor.

A Better Life

A New Social Class

The Renaissance saw the emergence of a new social class, tied to the economic activity of the cities. Still marginal during the Middle Ages, the bourgeoisie established its importance during the fifteenth and sixteenth centuries; it was the bourgeoisie that mastered the arts of commerce and the manufacture of goods; knew how to handle money and make it produce wealth; and made its way into the administration of the nascent states. Gradually gaining awareness of its role, the bourgeoisie developed its own culture and vision of the world. In a small book published in Florence during the fifteenth century, entitled *Advice Concerning Commerce*, a merchant addressed a young man who also meant to go into business: "Your help, your defense, your honor, your profit, these all lie in money. Money must circulate, and should never slumber in a coffer." "If you have money," advises another merchant, "do not let it lie sterile in your home, for it is better to act, even if the profit is small, than to lie passive, with no profit at all."

In Italy especially, thanks to their great wealth, the leading families of the urban aristocracy displayed their power by the building of palaces, patronage of the arts, and the decoration of chapels bearing their names. In Florence, the Tornabuoni family had itself depicted in frescoes in the chapel of the choir of the basilica of Santa Maria Novella, painted by Domenico Ghirlandaio, portraying stories of the lives of the Virgin Mary and John the Baptist. Cosimo de' Medici employed a portion of his immense wealth to build a sumptuous palace, renovate and rebuild the church of San Lorenzo, and found the Dominican monastery of San Marco. Much the same went on, during the fifteenth century, with the Rucellai,

1

2

Strozzi, and Pitti families. This magnificent behavior recurred in France with merchants such as Jacques Coeur, and in Germany with the Fuggers. Across Europe, but especially in Italy, it became customary for great families to build magnificent country villas, residences that clearly stood apart from those of the peasants and farmers, built for enjoyment and pleasure, embodying the architectural language of the Renaissance: porticoes, colonnades, monumental stairways, and enormous reception halls. Likewise, numerous wealthy members of the bourgeoisie purchased lands surrounding the cities, often in the hopes of acquiring a lordship, meaning a title of nobility and membership in the aristocracy.

Alongside this wealthy aristocracy, however, was the vast array of conditions of the petty bourgeoisie, who, little caring for lavish ostentation, saved its money, invested wisely, conducted business prudently, and pursued the professions of the law and technical skill. In those circles, what counted was love of family, domestic comfort, the education of the children, the value of work well done, and an active role in community affairs. A model of life that developed in northern Europe, and which began to appear in paintings, by Flemish artists at first, and later by Dutch painters.

4

3

The affirmation of the bourgeoisie went hand in hand with a development in domestic living, and paintings, from Italy to Flanders, showed how individual values underwent a notable change in a brief period of time.

1. Filippino Lippi (1457–1504): The Virgin and the Saints, *detail; painting on wooden panel. Florence, Church of the Santo Spirito.*

2. Benedetto da Maiano (1442–1497): Pietro Mellini; *marble. Florence, Museo del Bargello.*

3. Lorenzo Lotto (1480–1556): Messire Marsile and his wife; *painting on wooden panel. Madrid, Prado.*

4. Joos Van Cleve (1485–1540): Portrait of a woman; *painting on wooden panel. Florence, Uffizi.*

Life in the Cities

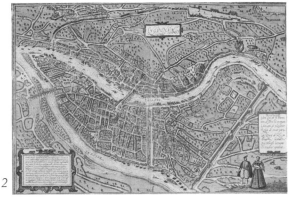

1

European cities in the Renaissance preserved traces of their medieval origins, in the monuments that symbolized them—cathedrals, bell towers, town halls, massive city walls—but also in the monasteries, convents, hospitals, and universities for which they were famed. Cities were also the capitals of the new professions of the law, practiced by notaries, prosecutors, lawyers, and judges. In some cases, cities were capitals of principalities, enriched by the presence of a court and a bureaucracy that grew together with a political power that was increasingly centralized and intolerant of rivals.

What determined the fortune of a town or city, however, was first and foremost the "mechanical workers," the craftsmen, masters, apprentices, and laborers. In different countries, they were organized variously into corporations or guilds, meant to ensure the quality of production and safeguard its diffusion, by codifying hierarchies and relationships and by preserving traditions. In general, a city presented a complete array of all trades and crafts, though certain cities did specialize, such as Ypres, in Flanders, in the weaving of cloth, or certain towns in Germany or Bohemia linked to mining. These thousands of men and women supported a population of merchants, bakers, butchers, and tavernkeepers, as well as a demi-monde of prostitutes, beggers, and thieves.

Slowly, cities changed during the fifteenth and sixteenth centuries. They benefited from the effects of a newly dynamic economy, stimulated by technological progress in the textiles industry, by improvements

The cities of the Renaissance were marked, like those of the Middle Ages, by an urban organization in which the various quarters were determined, variously, by the parish church at which they worshipped, the types of trades practiced, and by the geographic—and occasionally, the religious—origins of the residents. Most cities had quarters of butchers, weavers, and goldsmiths; often there was a Lombard quarter or a Jewish ghetto. In Venice, the island of Giudecca is originally said to have taken its name from the religion of its inhabitants, originally from the Levant, beginning in 1516, in the quarter of the foundry ("ghetto," in Venetian dialect), the "German" Jews, who had often come from other Italian cities, were authorized to reside, governed by exceeding strict laws.

2

1. *Andrea Mantegna (1431–1506):* Prayer in the Garden of Gethsemane, *detail, painting on wooden panel. Tours, Musée des Beaux-Arts.*

2. *Plan of Lyons, taken from the* Civitates Orbis *by Braun, colored engraving from the sixteenth century. Florence, Biblioteca Nazionale.*

3. *Hendrik van Steenwyk (1550–1603):* Marketplace in the Low Countries; *painting on wooden panel. Aix-en-Provence, Musée Granet.*

4. *The atelier of the Parisian goldsmith Etienne de Laulne, in an engraving from the sixteenth century.*

in communications, and by the often contradictory effects of the flow of new money triggered by the arrival of gold and silver from the Americas. They cities also attempted to present a new face, with new, better constructed residences, broader and straighter streets. Glass began to appear in the windows of the houses; eye-witness accounts state that half of the homes in Vienna had glass windows by the middle of the fifteenth century. The city was now also the realm of knowledge, because of the venerable universities long located there, but also because of the schools and colleges that were being founded, triggering a spread in literacy that in some cases reached from a third to a half of the inhabitants.

The Ideal City

Whatever projects of embellishment and reclamation might have been undertaken to the structure of old cities, an ideal city could not exist in direct contact with relics of the past. In the views of the theorists of the Renaissance, and for the builder-princes, the ideal city had always to be built *ex nihilo*, or from scratch. The ideal city demanded a regular design that, alone, would allow the successful coordination among the various spaces and their functions: be they military, commercial, artisanal, or political. The city of Renaissance dreams could only be built on virgin land. In France, the first experiments involved projects for the construction of fortresses and ports, and they came about at the behest of Francis I, who summoned Italian architects to design and build them. In 1545, he commissioned the Bolognese engineer Girolamo Marini to do the work at Vitry-le-François. The

work at Le Havre was assigned to the Siennese architect Bellarmato who, according to a royal letter dated June 1541, was expected to "oversee the construction and building of said town, port, and harbor, and to decorate and adorn them with both fortifications and handsome buildings, broad roads, and houses built and finished in accordance with a design that was commanded by us, following the advice of certain individuals with great experience in this field." We see various ideas developing, such as that of sweeping perspectives to provide enjoyment for the eyes, and the construction of a shared cistern and underground escape

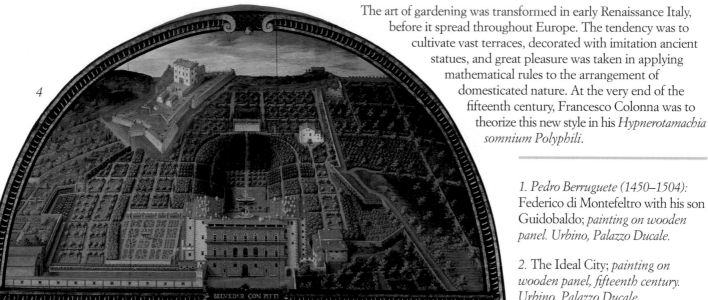

The art of gardening was transformed in early Renaissance Italy, before it spread throughout Europe. The tendency was to cultivate vast terraces, decorated with imitation ancient statues, and great pleasure was taken in applying mathematical rules to the arrangement of domesticated nature. At the very end of the fifteenth century, Francesco Colonna was to theorize this new style in his *Hypnerotamachia somnium Polyphili*.

1. Pedro Berruguete (1450–1504): Federico di Montefeltro with his son Guidobaldo; *painting on wooden panel. Urbino, Palazzo Ducale.*

2. The Ideal City; *painting on wooden panel, fifteenth century. Urbino, Palazzo Ducale.*

3. Antonio Averlino, known as Il Filarete (1400–1469): Plan of the city of Sforzinda, imagined for the Sforza family; drawing taken from the "Trattato di Architettura." Florence, Biblioteca Nazionale.

4. Justus van Utens (sixteenth century): The Pitti Palace, the Gardens of Boboli, and the Fort of Belvedere; painting on wooden panel. Florence, Museo di Firenze Com'Era.

5. Bernardino Gaffuri (sixteenth century): Piazza della Signoria, with the monument to Cosimo I; inlay. Florence, Museo degli Argenti.

routes for the safety and well-being of the inhabitants. The example had arrived from Italy, where the concept of ancient forums was reborn, classical squares with a complete architectural vocabulary made up of pediments and columns, pilasters and porticoes. In Ferrara, in 1494, the Duke of Este, Ercole I, undertook an operation of urban construction on a level that Italy had not seen since Roman times. The city was transformed, with new quarters, squares, and prestigious sites; at the same time, there were streets lined with modest, one-story homes, inhabited by craftsmen. During the same years, in Urbino, Federico di Montefeltro built a new cathedral, laid out a parade ground, and ordered the construction of a palace complex, looking out over the town and dominating the countryside, impressive from the exterior and charming on the interior, nicely furnished for comfortable living, and equipped with vast cellars and model stables.

A Better Life

Countryside and Peasants

1

In the family tree running from the Jacquerie of 1358, down to the movement of the Tuchins or that of the peasants of Kent of the 1380s, the countrysides of the fifteenth and sixteenth centuries were still periodically shaken by peasant revolts, more-or-less organized protests on the part of the rural populations against the miseries of the time. In this period of religious doubt and growing power of the state, the peasant movements took on variously religious and national connotations, as was the case with the uprising of the Hussites in Bohemia during the fifteenth century. The peasant revolts in Germany, from which Luther was forced to dissociate himself in 1525, were also not distant from this atmosphere.

The countryside of the Renaissance continued to suffer from three afflictions of the low Middle Ages: plague, war, and famine. The plague—though no epidemic provoked anything like the appalling hecatomb of 1348—returned regularly to mow down the inhabitants of city quarters, villages, and hamlets, disappearing for a while and then returning later, sparing one region and wreaking havoc in another. War, unpredictable and savage, might variously leave some lands intact or brutally ravage others, depending on the route of march for the armies, the agreements or conflict among monarchs, or various civil struggles. At the end of the fourteenth century and during the following century, the miseries of war were visited in particular upon Italy and certain provinces that were being harshly battled over by the king of France and the Holy Roman emperor. Savoy, Lorraine, and Artois thus fell regularly victim to warfare, struggling to exist under the permanent threat of invasion. Famine, on the other hand, did not seem to threaten the West as it had in the past, but food was still scarce whenever there were poor harvests, caused either by bad weather or human violence. Harvests, while remaining relatively small, progressed slightly all over Europe. In some areas, food crops were alternated with fodder crops, and this improved the fertility of the land; in other areas, entirely new crops appeared, such as rice in the Milanese region. Working the land remained, for the most part, a sustenance activity; in a growing number of areas, however, peasants were beginning to raise crops that yielded revenues: grapes, livestock, plants that yielded textiles

2

3

or dyes. The cultivation of woad—a plant that was used to make a blue dye—developed in the region around Toulouse; woad then began to dwindle, making way for corn, a new arrival from the Americas, hemp in Brittany or around Padua, and linen in Lombardy. The mulberry tree became common in the climates suited to it; the demand for silk far outstripped the supply. The cultivation of the mulberry tree was even encouraged by the authorities; for instance, the Silk Guild in Florence persuaded the Seignory in 1440 to require every rural estate of a certain size to plant fifty mulberry trees. Likewise, the olive tree established itself in Tuscany and Liguria, as did the orange tree in Sicily. New areas of cereal production appeared in Poland and the Baltics. Marketed by Dutch merchants, these "wheats" (in reality, they were forms of rye) were sold in the various ports of the North Sea, competing with the crops of Picardy, Hainaut, and Artois. These commercial exchanges spread to the rest of Europe, working deep-seated changes in the rural world, which was increasingly opening up to the cash-based economy. More than ever, the wealth of the countryside depended on the wealth of the cities; the best cultivated and most prosperous countryside was that surrounding a city.

1. School of Fontainebleau (sixteenth century): Threshing wheat; *painting on wooden panel. Paris, Musée du Louvre.*

2. Alessandro Allori (1535–1607): Sowing seeds; *drawing. Florence, Gabinetto dei Disegni e delle Stampe.*

3. Pieter Bruegel the Elder (1528–1569): Haymaking; *painting on wooden panel. Prague, National Gallery.*

A Better Life

New Ways of Life?

1

The rural world, increasingly interconnected; the cities, more and more linked up by the network of trade; the bourgeoisie, ever more numerous, powerful, and triumphant—all these factors brought about modifications in everyday existence. Of course, villages continued to live to the sound of church bells, which punctuated all of the ordinary moments and phases of life, the festivals and the dangers—from the majestic tolling of funerals, to the frenetic clanging of alarm. The simple fact of belonging to a parish or a community of villagers in time turned into a form of local patriotism, and there were numerous conflicts with neighboring farms, as hostility toward strangers spread and sank its roots. The Middle Ages had been a time of wandering, but from the fifteenth century on, strangers were no longer considered pilgrims or paupers—whom the church directed good Christians to aid and comfort—but rather intruders, to be driven away, or at least mistrusted.

While opening up to the new possibilities of accumulating wealth, the rural world clung ever more tightly to its habits, customs, and routines. Some even regretted the new developments. In 1547, in

1. Chiaveghino (1550–1613): The Charity of Saint Facio, *detail; canvas. Cremona, Ospedale Maggiore.*

2. Giuseppe Arcimboldo (1527–1593): Summer; *painting on wooden panel. Paris, Musée du Louvre.*

3. Bowl of fruit, in majolica; sixteenth century. Faenza, Museo della Ceramica.

4. Flemish knife with inlaid handle; silver and mother-of-pearl, sixteenth century. Florence, Museo del Bargello.

5. Veronese (1528–1588): The Wedding at Cana, *detail; canvas. Paris, Musée du Louvre.*

2

3

4

5

The culinary arts were increasingly important in court life during the Renaissance, and treatises on the subject began to appear. Cooking had changed relatively little since the Middle Ages, but food was served in a more refined manner, and seasoned with new spices.

his work *Propos Rustiques*, the Frenchman Noël du Fail criticized the frequent use of spices and new condiments: "No one has a banquet anymore without spices and other such foolishness, brought from the cities to our villages, which do not nourish the bodies of men, but rather corrupt them and add nothing to them." The same author rejects the excessively gentle mores which seemed to govern relations between men and women; fantasizing a bit, he evokes olden days, when a gallant male, "having said a sweet nothing or two to Jeanne or Margot, and swiftly looking around to make sure they were not observed, would grab her and, without a word, throw her down onto a bench, and the rest I leave to your imaginations." To this chronicler, the blame for the general flaccidity of customs, the disappearnace of simple and virile tastes, both at table and in lover's lane, was easy to attribute. It was the city that produced deleterious influences upon the countryside, and beneath the playful tone of his writing hides a nascent opposition, destined to grow and flourish, between city and country. The new economic circuits were especially helpful to a peasant "aristocracy," farmer-laborers that constituted rural dynasties, surviving from lease to lease, and in some cases even owning their own lands. These *coqs de village*, or "village roosters," common especially in the wealthier regions, helped to maintain relations with the authorities, dominated the poorer peasants, and owned plows, harrows, rollers, and light carts, which they rented to their less-wealthy neighbors. And while serfdom had almost completely vanished, those who possessed nothing more than the strength of their back, the "sharecroppers" who rented themselves out year by year or who simply worked the fields, had an increasingly hard time of it, with prices rising faster than their pay. It has been calculated that, during the fifteenth century, in many French regions, the purchasing power of farm workers diminished by a third, and in some cases by half.

The fifteenth and sixteenth centuries saw the introduction of many new plants, some from the Far East and others from the Americas. The mulberry tree was introduced to Tuscany from China, in 1434, and then spread throughout Southern Europe. The artichoke and the cauliflower made their first appearance, and the carrot and the strawberry were domesticated. Corn became more popular during the sixteenth century, but plants from the Americas were relatively limited, since the tomato and the potato were not adopted until later.

The Family, Women, and Children

Ideas about childhood, women, and the family changed in the fifteenth century, and especially the sixteenth century. Despite frequent epidemics and the spectre of death always on the prowl, the family circle expanded. It was no longer a rare occurrence for grandparents to see their grandchildren, and if old women were considered so repulsive by the men of the Renaissance, that was partly because it was no longer uncommon actually to meet many of them in both city and countryside.

On the other hand, young and lovely women became so much the object of male attentions and yearning that a full-fledged sexual revolution took place; the Protestant Reformation and its counterpart, the Catholic Counter Reformation, took several decades to overcome these new freedoms and to establish a new sexual order. Poets and painters glorified the female body, unisex public baths were very popular, and village dances were opportunities for debauchery. Erotic themes were explored by writers and poets; Giovanni Boccaccio and Pierre de Brantôme owed their popularity to these topics, as did thousands of authors of light-hearted fables and the anonymous coiners of salacious proverbs. Rome was renowned for its courtesans, proverbially accommodating to pilgrims far from home. In Venice a guidebook listing the local ladies of the night had 215 names with specialties and prices. Women both frightened men and attracted them, for the sensuality attributed to them. Montaigne rejoiced in that sensuality: "They easily lend themselves to pleasure"; elsewhere, he takes offense: "Even those women who are drained of bodily strength by age, still quiver, whinny and shudder with love." In some cases, women also claimed the right to love and pleasure, as in this ditty by Louise Labé:

Kiss me again, kiss me and kiss me
Give me your most flavorful kisses
Give me your most amorous kisses:
And I will return them, hotter than embers.

1. *Andrea della Robbia (1435–1525):* Head of young woman; *high relief in glazed terracotta. Florence, Museo del Bargello.*

2. *Hairpin adorned with two figures embracing; ivory, fifteenth century. Bologna, Museo Civico.*

3. *Leonardo da Vinci (1452–1519):* Child with a cat; *drawing (facsimile). Florence, Gabinetto dei Disegni e delle Stampe.*

4. *Bronzino (1503–1572):* Eleonora of Toledo and her son John; *painting on wooden panel. Florence, Uffizi.*

5. *Andrea della Robbia (1435–1525):* Medallion with a "putto"; *high relief in glazed terracotta. Florence, Ospedale degli Innocenti.*

6. *Giovan Francesco Caroto (1480–1555):* Child and drawing of a puppet; *painting on wooden panel. Verona, Museo di Castelvecchio.*

1

2

3

A response is offered by Erasmus, defender of the institution of marriage: "The greatest joy lies not in bed. That joy can be found in the profound union of two souls, in mutual trust, in the reciprocal cultivation of the virtues. Love does not always outlive the first kisses. But if it is Christian love, it triumphs in the decline of the body." These concepts made way for similar feelings about children, at least among the well-to-do bourgeoisie. Children appear in paintings, and gradually acquire an identity all their own. They have their own world, language, and education which must be tended to; they occupy a growing space, and the death of a child causes enormous grief. In the words of the Polish poet Kochanowski upon the death of his daughter at age four: "And you, my consolation, you will never be restored to me in all the centuries and you will not come to put a halt to my languishing grief."

5

4

Beginning in the fifteenth century, it was not uncommon to see children appear alongside their parents in paintings, the sign of a greater attention to childhood, and clearly the mark of a shift in emotional ties within the family. This tendency was confirmed in another sense by the greater care given to orphans and foundlings. The institutions devoted to their care multiplied in number in the cities, especially in Italy, as in Florence, for instance, with the Ospedale degli Innocenti.

6

Northern Europe

Excluded, at least for a period of time, from the lands across the ocean, unable to keep pace with the Iberian peninsula in trans-Atlantic trade, northern Europe—from England to the Baltic, from the Low Countries to Germany, and from Scandinavia to Poland—continued to engage in intense economic activity. Hansa, or the Hanseatic League (a confederation of roughly a hundred ports and towns, bound—despite various rivalries—by common interests, linked by a shared language and by various elements of civilization), ensured continuous trade between northeastern Europe and western and southern Europe. This trade comprised exchanges of wood, wax, furs, and rye from the north, for the salt, cloth, and wine of the Atlantic ports. All the same, these heavy goods brought in only a modest profit (barely 5 percent) and Hansa, whose economy still hovered between barter and cash, entered a slow decline.

Inland German cities were described by travellers as vast and lovely metropolises, such as Vienna, Cologne, Augsburg, or Nuremberg. The latter city, industrious and bustling with commerce, was also a financial marketplace, strategically situated between Venice and Antwerp, the Mediterranean and the Atlantic. Flanders remained by far the most industrious region in the West, with an unrivaled textiles industry, well-stocked fairs, and prosperous agriculture.

In the wake of the Black Death, the population of London plunged to just 20,000. Recovery followed, and London, thanks to its trade with the merchants of the Hanseatic League, grew with a certain energy. But it was not until the sixteenth century that the city acquired its standing as a great city of the West. At the end of the Renaissance, an even more spectacular period began for London: the Elizabethan era and the founding, in 1600, of the East Indies Company.

1

2

3

4

Bruges, with its 100,000 inhabitants in the year 1500, symbolized the region; this thriving port traded regularly with Lübeck, London, and Bordeaux, and received frequent shipments from Genoa (from 1277 on), and from Venice beginning in 1314. The splendor of Bruges's churches, monasteries, convents, houses, and squares was renowned throughout Europe; equally famous were the city's artists, among them Van Eyck and Memling. Still, Bruges, at the peak of its prosperity, was threatened as Flemish drapery lost its position of preeminence; even more insidious was the losing battle against the silting up of its outer harbors.

Antwerp in turn began to prosper; Amsterdam also started to develop. In the last year of the fifteenth century, the "factor," or trade representative of the king of Portugal took up residence in Antwerp, and it was here that the remarkable economic enterprise of the Portuguese first touched northern Europe. German merchants, previously forced to travel all the way to Venice in search of "spices and drugs," began to acquire their provisions in Antwerp, paying with their well-cast "thalers," a coinage that was much in demand in the marketplaces of Europe. The city, moreover, was more than just a port, it was also a manufacturing center. As early as 1559, Antwerp boasted nineteen sugar refineries.

1. Jan Bruegel the Elder (1568–1625): Landscape with Windmill. *Moscow, Pushkin Museum.*

2. Hans Memling (1440–1494): The Mystical Marriage of Saint Catherine, *detail; painting on wooden panel. Bruges, Memling Museum.*

3. Pieter Bruegel the Younger (1564–1637): Country Dance; *painting on wooden panel (after Pieter Bruegel the Elder). Florence, Uffizi.*

4. Joachim Patenier (1485–1524): The Flight into Egypt, *detail; painting on wooden panel. Madrid, Prado.*

A Better Life

Eastern Europe

In many ways, eastern Europe was cut out of the mainstream of the Renaissance. Moscow, during the fifteenth and sixteenth centuries, was light-years away from the splendors of Italy or the court of France, and the living conditions of peasants did not improve as they had in the West. Still, during this period, on the eastern fringes of the European continent, changes were occurring that would mark the history of the centuries that followed. In

Russia, a new state began to form around the grand principality of Muscovy which claimed roots in the Byzantine tradition; with Ivan II this principality took the town of Moscow as its capital. Ivan III (1462–1505) strove to make the city a testimonial to his power and wealth, and by the time of Ivan IV "the Terrible" (1533–1584), this ambition to found a new empire had grown to the point that he awarded himself, in 1547, the title of "Caesar," or Czar. He also commemorated his victories in the cityscape of Moscow; the church of Saint Basil, across from the Kremlin, was built to exalt his glory. His overriding concern was eastward expansion, and Cossacks and Russian merchants came to dominate Siberia. Waves of peasant colonization pushed as far as the Urals and the Volga, consolidating the triumphs of military expeditions.

In the sixteenth century, Russia also began to turn westward, opening up to the kingdoms of England and France and the merchants of Holland, taking its place in the European political and social landscape.

Poland, to the west of Russia, carried on a victorious struggle during the fifteenth century to resist the expansion of the Germanic states of the Teutonic Order, and then allied itself through a fortunate dynastic conjunction with the state of Lithuania, under the leadership of the Jagiello dynasty. King Sigismund I (1506–1548) ruled Poland during this fortunate period, an enlightened and humanist ruler. The University of Krakow thus became one of the great European centers of science, and boasted Copernicus among its scholars.

Ivan IV the Terrible maintained a two-fold image, that of a cruel sovereign and that of one of the great founders of Russian might. Thanks to him, Russia—which was no longer the little Muscovy which his father, Ivan III, had transformed into a full-fledged centralized state—became a member of the group of European nations. By modernizing and beautifying Moscow, which at the time of his reign had a population of 100,000, by endowing the city with printing presses and new quarters, by giving his state access to the sea, he showed the breadth of his understanding and the depth of his political vision. At the same time, he set out to savagely repress the feudal powers of the old aristocracy, with a limitless cruelty that manifested itself as well in fits of murderous rage to which even his son finally fell victim.

The real danger—once the Germanic threat had been warded off, however temporarily, and domination had been established over Hungary, Bohemia, and Moldavia—came from the east, where Muscovy was growing steadily stronger, spreading westward and along the coasts; another threat came from Sweden, at the end of the sixteenth century, with the continental ambitions of the Wasa dynasty. Poland thus found itself pushed into the traditional dilemma of a state surrounded by major expansionist powers, and the century that followed would be one of the most difficult in its history.

EASTERN EUROPE IN 1559

3

1. *The cathedral of Saint Basil, in Moscow, sixteenth century.*

2. *Plan of Moscow, taken from the "Urbium precipuarium mundi theatrum"; colored engraving, seventeenth century. Genoa, Museo Navale di Pegli.*

3. *Ignazio Danti and Stefano Buonsignori (sixteenth century):* Map of Muscovy; *panel from a cabinet. Florence, Palazzo Vecchio.*

A Better Life

Feasts and Lavish Display

From princely courts to the humblest villages, the feast was a year-round presence. Religious feasts, where the church and the faithful set out all the lavish display of faith. Feasts that were virtually profane, feasts of mid-Lent or feasts of the fires of Saint John. Feasts of crop harvests or vintage feasts, marking the gathering of grapes, and "kermis" feasts in northern Europe. And there was even the feast of lovers, the 14th of February, Saint Valentine's Day, which had already long been celebrated throughout Italy. There were royal feasts to mark the "joyous entry" of a sovereign into a city or town following a military victory, or the sumptuous reception of a visiting foreign prince.

  The days of Carnival continued the tradition of "masques," processions of floats or masquerades. In Florence or Venice, each guild or profession would field its own float, and the feast also served as an opportunity to make fun of one's fears, by scoffing at images of death. In Modena, for instance, the members of the Oratory of Death, dressed as skeletons, paraded down the street leading horses loaded with bones and skulls. Also popular were bulls set free in

1

Tournaments, holdovers from the traditions of medieval chivalry, remained fashionable during the Renaissance, and some sovereigns were devoted to them, including Francis I and Henry VIII. Henri II was to die during a joust, on June 30, 1559, upon the lance of Montgomery.

1. Antonio Tempesta (1555–1630): Tournament in Piazza Castello; *painting on wooden panel. Turin, Galleria Sabauda.*

2. Pieter Balten (1525–1598): Village Fair; *painting on wooden panel. Cremona, Museo Civico.*

3. Niccolò dell'Abate (1509–1571): Game of Tarots; *fresco. Bologna, Palazzo Poggi.*

4. Spectacle in the courtyard of the Pitti Palace; *engraving, sixteenth century. Florence, Gabinetto dei Disegni e delle Stampe.*

town squares, horse races run through the streets of the town, and foot races. In Rome, races were run by Jews, others were run by old men; in Brescia, there was even a prostitute race. These were occasions not only for mockery but symbolic ceremonies of community integration.

Tourneys, violent games, and war games were all equally popular, and some of them were particularly cruel; for example, in Bologna, the "game of the cat" was held, where a man locked in a cage with a cat would try to kill the animal with his teeth, and without using his hands. In Venice, the most sumptuous feast took place on Ascension Day, marking the "wedding of the sea." Accompanied by a flotilla of boats, the patriarch of Venice would bless the tide and the doge would drop a golden ring into the water, symbol of an alliance that was crucial to the city's prosperity. Court life focused particularly on hunting, balls, entertainment, and banquets, where the diners would compete in witticisms, doing their best to shine; literature was greatly honored. The court of Isabella d'Este at Ferrara was renowned, as was the court of Marguerite de Valois, sister of Francis I. People played freely at seduction, and it was even possible to dedicate poems to the noble ladies present, including even the queen.

The great spectacles of the Renaissance were harbingers of the Baroque festivals in the century that followed. Theatrical productions and the feigned sea battles were held. They were grandiose productions, in which a square or a palace might become the setting for a remarkable and festive display in honor of whoever—most frequently a prince or high member of the nobility—was staging the celebrations.

4

The Devil and His Allies

Men and women of the Renaissance had beliefs, anxieties, fears, and superstitions that were not far removed from those of the preceding centuries, but they seemed to dread the forces of the occult even more intensely than had been the case in the Middle Ages. The fifteenth and sixteenth centuries witnessed the blossoming of a culture of the fantastic that placed considerable emphasis upon witchcraft.

In the second half of the fifteenth century all of Europe was swept by millennarian dreams and terror at a supposed impending Apocalypse. The end of the world was widely feared, and many waited in dread for the signs of the coming catastrophe: monstrous births, the fall of celestial bodies, or even bloody rainshowers. Inquisitors came to believe that the devil had his allies on earth, his henchmen, his satanic legions lurking in the larger mass of good Christians, and that he had chosen witchcraft as the prime means to battle the true faith, in the wake of the defeat of the various heresies. A bull issued by Pope Innocent VIII, *Summis desiderantes*, in 1484, confirmed this belief, and gave the highest priority to the battle against the henchmen of Satan. The *Martellum Maleficarum*, a manual for inquisitors, was widely read and followed; it described methods of interrogation, signs of guilt, and the proper scale of punishments. One century later, the Frenchman Jean Bodin in his book *Demonology* (1581) listed the crimes commited by sorcerers: "They reject God. They curse His name. They worship the Devil. They dedicate their children to him. They sacrifice their children to the Devil, before they can be baptized. They consecrate their children to Satan even before they leave their mothers' wombs. They promise the Devil that they will lure all that they are able into his service. They swear by the name of the Devil. They murder people, by poison and by enchantment. They cause livestock to die. They cause crops to wither. They engage in carnal knowledge with the Devil."

Suspicion focused on any unusual form of behavior, and especially came to rest on women, thought to be satanic creatures. Old women were frightening; young women had the "beauty of the devil." It was women who knew the secrets of plants and who had handed these secrets down, generation to generation, over

Another category of people continued to cause a sense of fear in the cities of the Renaissance— the poor. Urban life in this period was marked by the presence of an exceedingly unstable stratum of population, largely cut out of the usual circuits of charity and social integration, such as the parish churches or the guilds, nomadic, often drifting from town to town in search of the rare opportunities of a life of misery.

1. Marcantonio Raimondi (1480–1534): The Dance of Witches and Sorcerers; *engraving. Florence, Gabinetto dei Disegni e delle Stampe.*

2. Hieronymus Bosch (1450–1516): Triptych of the Garden of Earthly Delights, *right panel, detail; painting on wooden panel. Madrid, Prado.*

the centuries; the inquisitors would invariably find evidence of blameworthy activity in all that related to the old traditions of magic surviving in the countryside. Among those traditions was the use of *Datura stramonium*, or jimson weed, a medicinal plant with hallucinogenic properties; it was employed in the preparation of ointments applied to the skin, and, when swallowed, was clearly the source of the fantasy of flying on a broomstick to take part in the Black Sabbath, a recurrant image that embodies the dreams, unconfessed desires, and nightmares of the time.

Proceedings against those found guilty were not subject to appeal; punishment was harsh. In 1595, Nicolas Rémy, poet and private adviser to the duke of Lorraine, wrote: "Judges, show no fear in demonstrating severity in the arrests of sorcerers. The ages will praise these acts of justice." As he wrote these words, tens of thousands of victims had already been burnt at the stake; and an estimated 500,000 to two million persons met a similar fate from the fifteenth to the eighteenth centuries.

2

During the course of the
second half of the sixteenth
century, it seemed that the
favorable period that the
West had experienced
following the disappearance
of the recurring plagues of
the second half of the
fourteenth century had
come to an end, and that
the return of those epidemics
and crises was at hand. The
"lovely sixteenth century"
seemed to give way to a
period that, while admittedly
not as bleak as the reign of
terror of two centuries
previous, was certainly a
time of neither optimism nor
security. Agricultural
production was dealt a series
of setbacks, and numerous
fields were affected
negatively, even the arts.

*Pieter Bruegel the Elder
(1528–1569):* The Triumph of
Death; *painting on wooden
panel. Madrid, Museo del Prado.*

The Crisis of the Christian World

For many centuries, the Church had avoided fractures and schisms, through the use, variously, of fire, sharp steel, and fine words. Thus the Church eradicated the heresies of the thirteenth century by urging the lords of northern France against the Albigensians of Languedoc, encouraging the work of Franciscans and Dominicans throughout Europe, and making the Inquisition an effective and terrifying weapon in its defense. During the sixteenth century, however, the entire edifice of the Apostolic Roman Church began to crack and crumble, with part of it collapsing entirely, and all of it being profoundly changed in the course of several decades.

It was not a lack of faith that provoked the crisis; on the contrary, it was a new spiritual quest, a response to the doubts and anguish of the time. The Renaissance loved life too dearly to look at death without fear. Depictions of the *danse macabre*, or dance of death, and the Last Judgment appeared in growing number on the walls of sanctuaries and chapels. The true horror that haunted this era was the brutal epidemics of plague, constantly lurking, and sweeping away 50,000 souls in Milan in 1484, before going on to strike Rome, Florence, and Bologna. In 1520, 40,000 died in Avignon, while 60,000 died in Lyons in 1560.

The Church offered no response to this sense of anguish. For many of the faithful, the clergy appeared corrupt and the pope himself an unworthy successor to Saint Peter, the first apostle. The pontiffs failed to notice that the new printing technology had made the Bible directly accessible to many Christians, and that its teachings had made readers dissatisfied with ceremonial rites and valueless sacraments. The Sacred Scriptures, now widely known and discussed, offered food for thought, while the sermons of an often ignorant clergy began to be scorned and rejected.

In the face of this muffled unrest, particularly deep-rooted in areas where printed books were common (the Rhine Valley, the Low Countries, the Ile-de-France, the region around Lyons, and London), the Papacy offered no response to the doubts of the faithful other than the practice of selling "indulgences." In exchange for hard cash, for alms or for gifts, preachers would offer either the certainty of entering paradise, or a reduction in the number of years in purgatory for the donor or for those close to him or her. These vendors of indulgences traveled through Germany saying that "just as soon as the silver tinkles into the alms box, the soul will take wing from the burning heat of purgatory." This was an easy way for the Vatican to deal with its short-term financial needs, but it was not the spiritual response so fervently awaited by countless Christians.

4

3

In the fifteenth and sixteenth centuries, the "abuses of the Church" were numerous: papal nepotism, lavish building in Rome financed by the sale of indulgences, and a war-mongering Papacy. At a time when the Bible was more widely read, too many priests still delivered sermons and rites in a Latin that they did not understand, and ignored the rules of priestly celibacy. The educated men and women of the towns of the north could no longer trust in a Church that was clearly incapable of responding to their needs. The spread of a modern form of worship was the first step toward putting the individual and his faith at the center of all concerns. Bible study groups outside of the Church proper became more common.

1. Flemish painter of the sixteenth century: Lot and His Daughters, *detail; painting on wooden panel. Paris, Musée du Louvre.*

2. Danse Macabre, German woodcut of the late fifteenth century.

3. Hans Baldung Grien (1484–1545): The Knight, the Young Woman, and Death; *painting on wooden panel. Paris, Musée du Louvre.*

4. Bartholomaeus von Bruyn the Elder (1493–1555): Memento Mori; *painting on wooden panel. Saint Petersburg, The Hermitage.*

Religion and Beliefs

The Reformation

Like many of his time, a German monk in the town of Wittenberg, Martin Luther, was scandalized by the practice of selling "indulgences." On October 31, 1517, he publicly set forth 95 "theses," some of them attacking the authority of the pope. Despite stern admonitions from Rome, he renewed his criticism in 1520 and, in his zeal to reform the church, took the radical step of rejecting the sacraments (save for those of baptism and the Eucharist), as well as the worship of saints and the celibacy of priests.

Leo X issued a papal bull against the rebel priest; in response, Luther burned the text of the bull in the main square of Wittenberg on December 10, 1520. This act marked a definitive break; the fractious monk was excommunicated the following year, and the emperor Charles V banished him from the Holy Roman Empire. All the same, far from being isolated, Martin Luther found himself surrounded by fervent Christians who shared his desire for reform. Some of them were men and women of the church, others were humble believers, while others still were rich and powerful, such as the elector of Saxony, who placed Martin Luther under his protection. This led to an outbreak of conflict and fighting, after which Charles V found himself forced to allow each prince to choose between Rome and the new faith. When the emperor tried to take back these concessions, the Lutheran states and towns underwrote a "Protestation" and joined forces. In the face of widespread revolt, Charles V was forced to accept that the Germanic Holy Roman Empire was already split up among Catholics and Protestants.

Everywhere else in Europe, Luther's views were spreading, prompting discussion, and variously acceptance and rejection. Everywhere, there was

John Calvin (1509–1564), born in Picardy, studied first in Paris, and later in Orléans and Bourges, where he came into contact with humanist and Lutheran doctrines. After a first condemnation of his writings in 1533, he published *Institutes of the Christian Religion* in Latin in 1536.

---

1. Lucas Cranach the Elder (1472–1553): The Sermon, *detail of the Altar of Reformation; painting on wooden panel. Wittenberg, Parish church.*

2. Frontispiece of the first edition of the Bible in Luther's translation, 1534.

3. Lucas Cranach the Elder (1472–1553): Frederick the Wise, *elector of Saxony, surrounded by Reformers; painting on wooden panel. Plymouth, City Museum.*

4. Portrait of Calvin; canvas, sixteenth century. Geneva, Bibliothèque Universitaire.

3

4

excitement and agitation, especially in the cities. In France, John Calvin extended Luther's work and dreamt of founding a "city of God"; he felt he had found that city in Geneva, where he seized control in 1541 and rigorously applied the principles of the new religion, outlawing both "free-thinkers" and "papists."

In England, for reasons that were both personal and bound up with an underlying desire to be independent of Rome, King Henry VIII favored the birth of a local church; this church preserved the pomp and gold of the Catholic church, while at the same time adopting the foundations of a new form of spirituality offered by the Reformation. Thus came about the "Anglican" church, just as Europe was being riven by the terribles Wars of Religion.

Religion and Beliefs

103

The Wars of Religion

In France, from the beginning of the 1560s up to the Edict of Nantes (1598), or even up to the Peace of Alès (1629), Christians loyal to the Roman Catholic Church and supporters of the Protestant Reformation fought a bloody and seemingly endless series of battles, interrupted by various truces, and calling into question not only the religious orientation of the kingdom, but even the very foundations of the French monarchy. Religious affiliation, complicated by political questions, was also the cause of armed conflicts during the same period in numerous regions of Germany, in Bohemia, and in the Low Countries. The ideal of a unified Christendom vanished once and for all, and international rivalries found full expression in the battles among religious factions; Spain, for instance, supported the most ardent defenders of Catholic fundamentalism in France.

In France, the country where, without doubt, the state was most seriously shaken by a struggle that pitched the leading families of the realm one against the other, the first bloodshed dated back to 1562, with the massacre of the Protestants of Vassy by the men of the Duke of Guise. In a kingdom in which roughly a fifth of the population had converted to Protestant ideas, including

1

2

Catherine de' Medici (1519–1589), wife of the Duke of Orléans, became queen of France when her husband succeeded to the throne under the name of Henri II. Following his death, and during the reigns of her three sons, Francis II, Charles IX, and Henri III, she became the most important figure at the French court. Her determination to preserve the French monarchy led her to concede liberties to the Protestants (Edict of Amboise, 1563), as well as to give free rein to the most virulent Catholic extremists, resulting in the Massacre of Saint Bartholomew's Day, in which tens of thousands of French Protestants were murdered.

such great nobles as Condé and Coligny, the fighting went on for many decades, interrupted by edicts giving the Protestants greater or lesser numbers of safe havens. In 1572, the Massacre of Saint Bartholomew's Day marked the high point of violence.

The death of the Duke of Anjou, brother of King Henri III, in 1584 gave a new direction to the struggle: following the death of the king, the heir to the throne, Henri of Navarre, was the leader of the Protestants. The Catholics who most fiercely opposed this development, led by the Guise family and supported by Philip II, organized their opposition in the form of the Catholic League. In order to protect his kingdom from too great a danger—that of allowing Spain to dominate the French political scene—the most Catholic king Henri III ordered the assassination of the Duke of Guise; he himself was assassinated in 1589. It remained to Henri IV to conquer his own kingdom, and he did so gradually, aided by his abjuration of Protestantism, in 1593, and then by the Edict of Nantes which accorded freedom of worship and a certain degree of tolerance to the Protestants.

3

In the Holy Roman Empire under Charles V, Protestants and Catholics fought just as bitterly, and the attitude of the emperor varied in accordance with his commitments outside of Germany. In an empire whose population was by majority Lutheran, where princes used religion as a pawn in their struggles for power, the Peace of Augsburg ratified the end of conflicts that obeyed the principle *cujus regio, hujus religio,* Latin for "to each the religion of his or her prince."

1. Portrait of Catherine de' Medici; painting on wooden panel, sixteenth century. Florence, Museo Mediceo.

2. François Dubois (1529–1584): The Saint Bartholomew's Day massacre; *painting on wooden panel. Lausanne, Musée Cantonal.*

3. The Church of Lyons; canvas, 1565 circa. Geneva, Bibliothèque Universitaire.

The Counter-Reformation

For the Roman Catholic Church, badly weakened by the Reformation, the objective of a Counter-Reformation—which, given its breadth and the way in which it profoundly transformed Catholicism, became a veritable Catholic Reformation—was attained, first and foremost, during the sixteenth century. In order to combat the spread of the ideas of the Reformation, the old tribunal of the Inquisition was established once again, in 1542, with the addition a few years later of the Index, designed to banish publications that went against Roman Catholic precepts. More important by far, however, was the approval, in 1540, by Pope Paul III, of the Company of Jesus founded by Ignatius of Loyola, who became a formidable weapon in the battle against the Reformation and for Catholic Reformation of the Church in the service of the Papacy.

The Council of Trent (1545–1563) marked one of the great moments of clarification of the teachings of the Church. During the council, Rome reaffirmed the points that would remain non-negotiable, such as the continuation of the cult of the saints and the value of images. The Church condemned the

Ignatius of Loyola (1491–1556), a Spaniard from the Basque country, began his career at the court of the viceroy of Navarre. After being wounded at the siege of Pamplona, he decided to devote his life to religion, studying first at Salamanca, then in Paris. With several friends, in the 1530s he entered the service of the pope to evangelize in the Holy Land. In 1540, his group of evangelists became the Company of Jesus, a new religious order with Ignatius as father superior. The first task the order assigned itself was hardly in line with the pope's expectations; in fact, it devoted itself to the Counter-Reformation.

Protestant tendency to justify faith alone, and reaffirmed the importance of the seven sacraments and the reality of the presence of Jesus Christ in Holy Communion. Lastly, the Roman Catholic Church worked to distance itself from the image that centuries of abuse had conferred upon it, by sharply improving the level of education of its priests, and entrusting them with the mission to Christianize the town and country, where religion still sank relatively shallow roots, and by attempting to repress—with varying degrees of energy and success—those situations that most grossly clashed with the principles of the Church, such as the cumulative awarding of benefices. Seminaries were founded, though not always with the hoped-for results; in any case the post-Tridentine Church was more worthy than the church that condemned Martin Luther. The Catholic church, following the Council of Trent, chose to emphasize these aspects, through a return to the tradition of processions, and, in a more general way, in a markedly Baroque art. Two religious orders, the Capuchins and the Jesuits, established prior to the council, found in these programs the instruments for a spectacular development, and became the most zealous promoters of the art and the message. In 1566, the *Tridentine Catechism* was published, and became the basic text in all questions of faith for centuries.

1. The Escorial; colored engraving from the sixteenth century, taken from the "Civitates Orbis" by Braun. Florence, Biblioteca Nazionale.

2. Alonso Sánchez Coello (1515–1590): Portrait of Philip II; *canvas. Madrid, Museo del Prado.*

3. Giovanni da Udine (1487–1535): The Council of Trent; *fresco. Vatican, Loggia della Cosmografia.*

3

Copernicus and Galileo: New Frontiers

STELLÆBURGUM · sive · OBSERVATORIUM · SUBTERRANEVM, A TYCHONE BRAHE Nobili Dano
IN INSULA HVÆNA, EXTRA ARCEM URANIAM. EXTRVCTVM · CIRCA · ANNVM · M · D · LXXXIIII.

1

When Galileo, in the 1620s, took up his research again in the face of the decree of 1616 that condemned the work of Copernicus, he felt that he could rely upon the protection of Cardinal Barberini, who had repeatedly encouraged his endeavors and who became pope in 1623 under the name of Urban VIII. But, beginning in 1624, this new pope demanded that Galileo show "objectivity," or, in other words, moderation in his new findings. Galileo failed or refused to understand these recommendations, and soon found himself subject to the rigors of the Holy Office. What followed was the famous trial, and the scientist's condemnation on June 22, 1633, followed by his kneeling abjuration of his beliefs about the Earth's orbit, and finally, the legendary muttered exclamation that followed: "*Eppur, si muove!*" (literally, "It still moves!")

2

During the Renaissance, broad new horizons opened out for science. The great discoveries and the major voyages of exploration pushed back the frontiers of the known world. The astronomic theories of Copernicus fit into a larger movement of expansions of the boundaries of knowledge, and at the end of the period, Galileo inaugurated a new era in the history of science.

Copernicus (1473–1543), a Pole who studied under Peuerbach at the University of Krakow, concentrated on trigonometry and its application to astronomy. He transferred in 1497 to the University of Bologna, and then traveled through Italy, from Padua to Ferrara and Rome. In 1503 he returned to Poland, and took up teaching again, attempting to overcome the limitations of the old Ptolemaic system, which underlay the Christian conception of the universe, with the Earth—a motionless ball—at the center of the celestial revolutions. He was able to show that the Earth does not lie at the center of the universe, and that it rotates on its own axis every 24 hours, and orbits the sun every 365 days; he was unable to publish these findings until he lay on his

3

4

deathbed, in 1543. Even though he dedicated his treatise *De Revolutionibus Orbium Coelestium* to Pope Paul III, the times were not ripe for this discovery to be accepted. Giordano Bruno, who also developed theories in this direction, paid for his intellectual daring with his life. Roughly a century later Galileo was hauled before the judges of the Holy Office.

Galileo Galilei (1564–1642), born at Pisa, moved at an early age to Florence. His studies completed, he became professor of mathematics at the University of Pisa, where he began to study the behavior of falling bodies. In 1592 he was appointed to a chair at the University of Padua. He then set out to perfect an instrument of observation invented in the Low Countries—the telescope—and began to use it to observe the sky. In 1610 he published *Sidereus Nuncius*, an account of his observations of the moon, the Milky Way, and especially Jupiter; Galileo demonstrated that Jupiter rotated, raising new questions about the Earth itself. Galileo then moved to Florence, under the protection of the Grand Duke Cosimo II de' Medici, but troubles began with the Church almost immediately. In 1616, Copernicus's work was banned by the Church, which indirectly forbade Galileo from questioning the "system of the world." Galileo refused to give up his studies, and in 1632 he published, in Italian, his *Dialogo sopra i due massimi sistemi del mondo*, in which he claimed that the Earth moved. He was condemned to indefinite imprisonment in 1633, and ended his life under house arrest in a villa at Arcetri near Florence; his famous *Discourses* were published in Leiden in 1638.

1. The observatory of Tycho Brahe, taken from the "Cosmographie Blaviane" by J. Blaeu; colored engraving, seventeenth century. Florence, Museo della Storia della Scienza.

2. Ottavio Leoni (1578–1608): Portrait of Galileo; drawing. Florence, Biblioteca Marucelliana.

3. Ceiling with astrological decorations; fresco, sixteenth century. Vatican, Sala Bologna.

4. Drawings by Galileo, illustrating the phases of the moon. Florence, Biblioteca Nazionale.

1453 Fall of Constantinople, stormed by the Turks; end of the Eastern Roman Empire. End of the Hundred Years' War.

1455 Gutenberg prints his first book, the Mainz Bible.

1461–83 Louis XI, king of France. He destroys the power of the great feudal lords and consolidates royal power. Upon his death, his kingdom coincides more or less with the territory of present-day France.

1462–65 The reign of Ivan III the Great is an important step in the creation of the Russian state.

1469 Lorenzo de' Medici, known as Lorenzo the Magnificent, becomes Seignior of Florence. Until **1478**, he governs with his brother Giuliano, who is assassinated in the conspiracy of the Pazzi family. Patron of the arts and letters, and himself a poet, he is the epitome of the image of the prince of the Renaissance. In Spain, the marriage of Isabella I of Castile to Ferdinand of Aragon lead to the unification of the two crowns, and facilitates the unification of Spain (completed in **1492** with the fall of the Moorish kingdom of Grenada).

1401 Lorenzo Ghiberti wins the competition for the second door of the Baptistery of Florence. Later (**1425–52**), he also designs and executes the third door, which Michelangelo was to call the *"Gate of Paradise."*

1420–36 Cupola of the Duomo, or cathedral, of Florence by Brunelleschi.

1427–28 In his fresco of the *Holy Trinity* in Santa Maria Novella in Florence, Masaccio applies the laws of perspective developed and perfected by Brunelleschi.

1433–43 Donatello, *David* (bronze).

1435 Leon Battista Alberti sets forth in *De pictura* the theory of geometric perspective.

1436 Fra' Angelico, *Annunciation.*

1452 Piero della Francesca, *The Story of the True Cross* (frescoes, Arezzo).

1478 Botticelli, *Primavera.*

1485 Botticelli, *The Birth of Venus.*

1494–97 Leonardo da Vinci, *The Last Supper.*

1495 Voyage in Italy of the German painter Albrecht Dürer.

1501–1504 Michelangelo, *David.*

1503–1507 Leonardo da Vinci, *La Gioconda,* or *Mona Lisa.*

1509 Raphael begins to decorate the great halls of the apartments of Julius II in the Vatican.

1514 Titian, *Sacred Love and Profane Love.*

1515 Succession of Francis I. He attracts to his court a great many artists, including Leonardo da Vinci, Benvenuto Cellini, and Primaticcio. The castles which he orders built or enlarged (such as Chambord, Azay-le-Rideau, and Amboise) clearly show the influence Italian architecture.

1536–41 Michelangelo, *Last Judgement.*

1546 Michelangelo supervises work on the cupola of Saint Peter's in Rome.

1550 Vasari writes les *Vite de' più eccellenti Pittori, Scultori e Architetti.*

1563 Veronese, *The Wedding at Canae.*

1594 Tintoretto, *The Last Supper* (San Giorgio Maggiore, Venice).

Facing page:
(top) *Luciano Laurana (1420–1479): Court of the Ducal Palace at Urbino.*

(bottom, left) *Masaccio (1401–1428):* Adam and Eve expelled from Paradise; *fresco. Florence, Brancacci Chapel, church of Santa Maria del Carmine.*

(bottom, right) *Donatello (1386–1466): Cantoria. Florence, Museo dell'Opera del Duomo.*

1477 The Low Countries fall under the rule of the Habsburgs.

1483 Reign of Charles VIII (1483–98). He lays claim to the rights of the house of Anjou over the kingdom of Naples. This marks the beginning of the wars of Italy. In 1494 Charles VIII marches into Italy and makes a triumphal entrance into Naples. The French are dazzled by the splendor of Italian civilization.

1485 End of the War of the Roses, between the houses of Lancaster and York. Succession of Henry VII, first of the Tudor line.

1492 Discovery of America by Christopher Columbus. Death of Lorenzo de' Medici.

1493 Maximilian I, German emperor. Due to his efforts to reorganize the Holy Roman Empire, he can be considered the true founder of the mighty Habsburg dynasty.

1495 At Fornovo, in Emilia Romagna, the League organized by Pope Alexander VI (Borgia) defeats the French army led by Charles VIII.

1498 The Dominican monk Girolamo Savonarola is excommunicated by

1304–1374 Petrarch's immense classical culture and his quest for ancient manuscripts, leads to his being considered the first great humanist of the Renaissance.

1380–1459 Poggio Bracciolini discovers numerous works of antiquity (Quintilian, Statius, Lucretius, Cicero).

1440 Cosimo de' Medici founds in Florence the Platonic Academy. Lorenzo Valla demonstates that the "Donation of Constantine" is a fake: philology becomes a tool with which to establish historical truth.

1453 After the fall of Constantinople, Byzantine scholars spread knowledge of ancient Greek throughout Europe.

1469 Marsilio Ficino begins to translate the works of Plato.

1486 Pico della Mirandola composes *De hominis dignitate.*

1497–1560 Melanchthon, professor of Greek at the University of Wittenberg, reconciles humanism and the Lutheran Reformation.

1511–16 Erasmus writes *In Praise of Folly,* Machiavelli writes *The Prince,* Thomas More writes *Utopia,* and Ariosto writes *The Orlando Furioso.*

1520 Lefèvre d'Etaples, translator of the Bible and of the work of Aristotle, creates the "Salon of Meaux."

1528 *The Courtier* by Baldassarre Castiglione exerts considerable influence in Europe.

1530 Francis I founds the Collège de France.

1532 Rabelais publishes *Pantagruel* and, two years later, *Gargantua.*

1549 Du Bellay writes the *Défense et Illustration de la Langue Française.*

1564 Birth of Shakespeare.

1575 Tasso completes *Jerusalem Delivered.*

1580–88 Publication of Montaigne's *Essais.*

1605–15 Cervantes publishes *Don Quixote.*

1616 Death of Shakespeare.

Alexander VI and burned at the stake for heresy in Florence. He had expelled the Medici from Florence and established a regime that was at once theocratic and democratic.

1499 *Peace of Basel:* the emperor Maximilian recognizes the independence of the Swiss cantons. Louis XII (**1498–1515**) organizes a new expedition into Italy, and conquers Milan, but by the treaty of Lyons (**1504**), he is obliged to recognize Spanish rule over southern Italy. In **1513**, the French are driven out of the Milan region.

1515 Francis I. This king was a patron of the arts, and attracted many great artists to his court. A true prince of the Renaissance, he lay the foundations for an absolute monarchy. Battle of Marignano.

1517 With his "95 theses," Luther denounces the sale of indulgences. Thus begins the Reformation.

André Thévet (1503/4–1592): Portrait of Gutenberg; *engraving. Strasburg, Cabinet des Estampes.*

Facing page: *Colantonio (Italian painter, active in Naples between 1440 and 1470):* Saint Jerome in his study, *detail; painting on wooden panel. Naples, Museo di Capodimonte.*

Chronology

1519 Charles V, master of an immense empire, altered the equilibrium in Europe. The great standoff with Francis V was thus practically inevitable. The theater of these lengthy wars was once again Italy.

1520–66 Soliman II the Magnificent undertakes an ambitious policy of conquest. The Ottoman Empire experienced the richest period in its history.

1525 Francis I is captured at the Battle of Pavia.

1527 The sack of Rome by the army of German landsknechts.

1529 Peace of Cambrai: Francis I renounces his claims to Italy and obtains Burgundy.

1531 Establishment of a commodities exchange in Antwerp: development of international finance.

1533–84 Ivan IV the Terrible takes the title of Czar of Russia (**1543**). He undertakes a vast administrative, legislative, religious, and military reorganization.

1534 *Act of Supremacy:* foundation of the Anglican church. Ignatius of Loyola founds the Company of Jesus.

1474 Dal Pozzo Toscanelli, Florentine geographer, asserts that the earth is spherical.

1492 Christopher Columbus discovers America.

1494 Treaty of Tordesillas: Spain and Portugal split up the New World.

1497 In the service of England, the Italian navigator John Cabot discovers Newfoundland and Labrador.

1497–98 Vasco da Gama discovers the route to the Indies around the Cape of Good Hope.

1499 Amerigo Vespucci undertakes numerous expeditions to the New World.

1500 Cabral discovers Brazil and claims it for Portugal.

1501 Beginning of the slave trade in America.

1505–15 Establishment of the Portuguese empire (East Indies, Goa, Malabar, Ormuz, coasts of Ceylon, Malacca).

1507 A German mapmaker uses the first name of Vespucci (Amerigo) to designate the new continent (America).

1519–21 First circumnavigation of the earth, by Magellan. The Spanish "conquistador" Hernando Cortés conquers and destroys the Aztec empire.

1523–35 Conquest of the Maya empire (central America).

1531–34 Pizarro conquers the Inca empire.

1535–36 The French navigator Jacques Cartier takes possession of Canada in the name of Francis I.

1546 Foundation of the city of Potosí (Bolivia), renowned for its silver mines.

1547 The Spanish monk Bartolomé de Las Casas denounces the horrors of colonization.

1564 Beginning of the Spanish occupation of the Philippines.

1584 Sir Walter Raleigh founds Virginia.

1600 Creation of the English East India Company.

1541 Calvin establishes a theocratic republic in Geneva.

1542 The Congregation of the Supreme Inquisition is founded in Rome.

1545–63 Council of Trent.

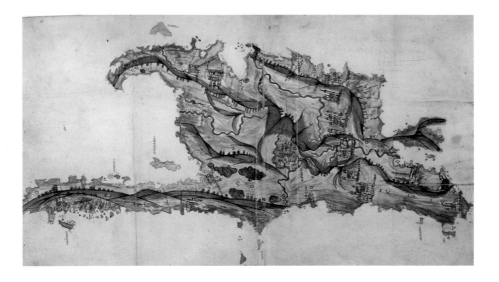

The island of Santo Domingo, in a Spanish map from the turn of the sixteenth century. Bologna, Biblioteca Universitaria.

Top: *Giorgio Vasari (1511–1574):* Portrait of Lorenzo the Magnificent; *painting on wooden panel. Florence, Uffizi.*

Facing page: The arrival of the Portuguese in Japan *(detail); screen; ink, paint, and gold on paper; Japan, Namban style, turn of the seventeenth century. Oporto, Musée Soares doa Reis.*

Chronology

Titian (1490–1576): Charles V on horseback. *Madrid, Museo del Prado.*

Facing page (top): *Abel Grimmer:* The Sermon. *Moscow, Pushkin Museum.*

(bottom): Saint Ignatius before Pope Paul III; *painting on wooden panel, sixteenth century. Rome, Church of the Gesù.*

1517 Luther denounces ("95 theses") the sale of indulgences. In **1520** he refuses to retract his condemnation, and publicly burns the papal bull *Exsurge Domine*, and publishes his main works: *Christian Nobles of Germany*, *On the Babylonish Captivity of the Church of God*, and *De servo arbitrio*. In **1522** he translates the New Testament into German.

1523 Zwingli imposes the Reformation in Zurich.

1524 Thomas Müntzer preaches an evangelical communism and instigates a peasant uprising in Germany. He is executed in **1525**.

1527 Gustav I introduces Lutheranism into Sweden. Christian III imposes the Protestant religion upon Denmark and Norway.

1534 Foundation by Loyola of the Company of Jesus, which became a protagonist of the Counter-Reformation and of the evangelization America and the Far East. Religious schism in England: with the Act of Supremacy, king Henry VIII becomes the chief of the Anglican church.

1535 Execution of Thomas More.

1541 In his *Christianae Religionis Institutio*, John Calvin sets forth the principles of his doctrine. He founds a theocratic republic in Geneva.

1542 The Catholic Church reorganizes the Tribunal of the Inquisition.

1545–69 Pope Paul III opens the Council of Trent in order to deal with the Protestant Reformation. Dogmas are examined and redefined, practices of worship are reaffirmed, the discipline of the clergy is reestablished, a new Catechism is drawn up, and an official version of the Sacred Scriptures is readied.

1562–1598 Wars of religion in France marked by atrocities (more than 3,000 die in the massacre of Saint Bartholomew's Day in **1572**). The Edict of Nantes signed by Henri IV gives the Protestants of France freedom of worship and offers them political, juridical, and military assurances.

1600 Giordano Bruno condemned by the Inquisition and burnt at the stake in Rome.

1616 The works of Copernicus are banned by the Index.

1633 Condamnation of Galileo.

1546 Death of Luther.

1547 Henri II succeeds Francis I. Edward VI (**1547–1553**) reinforces the Reformation in England.

1555 Peace of Augsburg: the Empire is split into Catholic and Lutheran sections, according to the principle of *cuius regio eius religio* (to each the religion of his prince).

1556 Abdication of Charles V, who gives his son, Philip II, Spain, the Low Countries, and Italy, and his brother Ferdinand the dominions of the Habsburgs. Rupture of the unity of the Holy Roman Empire.

1557 The vast flow of precious metals from the New World to Europe provokes widespread inflation and bankruptcy in Spain (**1557**) and Portugal (**1560**).

1559 The treaty of Cateau-Cambrésis puts an end to the wars of Italy.

1558–1603 Elizabeth I re-establishes the Anglican church, following the reign of the Mary I Tudor, also known as Bloody Mary. Spain loses its maritime supremacy. The Elizabethan era was a time

of enormous economic, commercial, and cultural development.

1560 In France, regency of Catherine de' Medici.

1562 Massacre of Wassy. Outbreak of the Wars of Religion in France.

1571 Battle of Lepanto. The Christian fleet of the Holy League (Spain, Venice, Holy See) routs the Turkish fleet.

1572 Massacre of Saint Bartholomew's Day.

1576 The Pacification of Ghent: unification of the Low Countries.

1579 Union of Utrecht: act of foundation of the Dutch Republic (Calvinist provinces).

1580 Annexation of Portugal by Philip II, king of Spain.

1578 Execution of Mary Stuart.

1588 The English fleet annihilates Spain's "Invincible" Armada.

1589 Assassination of Henri III, last king of the house of Valois, and succession of Henri IV of Bourbon, who abjures the Calvinist faith

and is consecrated king at Saint-Denis (1594).

1598 Edict of Nantes: freedom of worship for the Huguenots. End of the Wars of Religion.

Dome of the zodiac (planets and constellations during a night in July); fresco. Florence, the old sacristy of the church of San Lorenzo.

Facing page: (top) *Atelier of François Clouet: Henri II of Valois and Catherine de' Medici, surrounded by other members of the family; sixteenth century.*

(bottom) *Anatomic Theater of the University of Padua, end of the sixteenth century (used until 1872, it was the first of its kind in all Europe).*

■ SCIENCE AND TECHNOLOGY

1440 Gutenberg invents the printing press (movable type). Beginning in **1450** he perfects the machine and in **1455** publishes The Bible.

1460 Introduction of the blast furnace.

1470 Foundation of the Typographie de la Sorbonne; the first book is printed in France.

1494 Aldus Manutius founds a print-shop in Venice, renowned for its editions of the Greek and Latin classics. Luca Pacioli publishes a *Summa* of mathematical knowledge from antiquity on.

1516 Foundation at Saint-Etienne of the first factory for the manufacture of firearms.

1519 Leonardo da Vinci dies at Amboise.

A true "Renaissance man," he was a painter and architect, engineer and physicist, technician and inventer, anatomist and naturalist.

1531 Foundation of the silk industry in Lyons.

1541 Death of Paracelsus, physician and alchemist, who contributed to the development of chemistry.

1543 Vesalius writes an important treatise on anatomy. In *De revolutionibus orbium coelestium*, Copernicus develops the heliocentric theory.

1556 Georg Bauer, known as Agricola, systematically studies the minerals (*De re metallica*).

1559 The mathematician Cardano deepens the understanding of algebra.

1561 Birth of Francis Bacon, one of the creators of the experimental method.

1575 Publication of the works of Amboise Paré, considered the father of modern surgery.

1609–1619 The laws of Kepler confirm the hypothesis of Copernicus.

1632 In his *Dialogo sopra i due massimi sistemi del mondo*, Galileo sets forth all the evidence of the truth of the Copernican system. Galileo's discoveries in the fields of physics and astronomy open the way to modern science.

Chronology

The Château of Chambord, 1530.

Index

Index

Acknowledgments

*The photographs in this volume
all come from the
SCALA picture library in Florence, Italy
with the exception of the following:*

Archiv für Kunst und Geschichte, Berlin: 38, 74 (2), 102 (1-2)
Bibliothèque Nationale de France, Paris: 11
Claus Hansmann, München: 103 (3)
Gianni Dagli Orti, Paris: 36 (2), 39 (2), 43 (4), 44 (2), 45, 62 (1), 79 (3), 90 (2), 103 (4), 104 (2), 105, 115, 116
Istituto e Museo di Storia della Scienza, Florence: 108 (1)
Michel Pierre: 42 (2), 90 (1)

Maps by Roberto Simoni